248.8 Nor 12587

Northington, Jan, 1953-
Separated and waiting.

DISCARD

Arcade Baptist Church

12587

D0043576

Contents

Acknowledgments

I wish to thank Laree Brown for endless hours of typing and editing. Her suggestions and words of encouragement kept me going to the end. Without her efforts this book would not have been possible.

Introduction

Maybe you've picked up this book because you are separated and you're looking for help. Perhaps someone gave it to you thinking you could use some encouragement right now. Or if you're not separated, but someone dear to you is, you might be wondering what the person is going through right now. Ten years ago, when I was first separated, I looked desperately for a book that would help me work through this awkward space of time. I found plenty of books on how to make my marriage better or how to be reconciled. I found books on how to deal with divorce and how to survive as a single parent. But I found very little to help me survive separation.

No matter what this period of uncertainty is like for you—whether it came after many years of unhappiness or suddenly with no warning, whether it is long or short, whether it ends in reconciliation or divorce—I hope you will benefit from the uncertainties, fears, and struggles as well as the gift of healing I have to share. In addition to my experiences and reading, this book has grown out of the comments and insights of others. Over the years I've shared many friendships with separated individuals, and

I've attended numerous seminars and workshops for separated or divorced persons.

Don't panic if my experience and timetable for healing are not the same as yours, for we serve a patient God who allows and helps us to grow at our own rate. God loves you so much that He knows just what you need in your unique situation. But we do have pain and choices in common, and I hope to help you with them. I was separated—hurting and waiting for something—but I wasn't sure what it was. To be reconciled? Divorced? A single parent? A single adult? No, I was waiting to become God's trusting and maturing child. It was my choice.

I pray that God will use what I share in these pages, but above all, I pray that you will listen to what He says to you during this difficult time. His words will help because they will be the very ones you need. His words hold the power to heal and direct you. Healing won't take place overnight (just as the deterioration of your marriage didn't take place overnight), but don't despair. God doesn't design a pathway of ruin; He designs one of sure refinement. His refinement takes time: *waiting time*.

Your pain identifies you—your choices will direct you. The pain of separation identifies you right now, and you face some hard choices ahead. I'm sure you've heard of the two kinds of believers: those who wait on the Lord and those who keep the Lord waiting. One commentator observed, "Waiting is where we make the most important decisions we will ever make. In waiting, we decide what our attitude is going to be toward life itself. The activity of our hands is never more important than the ceaseless activity of a heart that is constantly choosing to wait, or not wait on the Lord."[1]

The Psalmist says:

I would have lost heart, unless I had believed
That I would see the goodness of the LORD. . . .
Wait on the LORD;
Be of good courage,
And He shall strengthen your heart;
Wait, I say, on the LORD! (Ps. 27:13–14).

Jesus said, "If you abide in My word, . . . you shall know the truth, and the truth shall make you free" (John 8:31–32). As I got to "know" the truth (which is Jesus), I discovered freedom: freedom from guilt, freedom to forgive people who had hurt me so deeply, freedom to love without expectations, and freedom to give to others.

My prayer is that this book will help prepare you for what lies ahead and offer you hope. There is hope—you can have freedom from your heart-wrenching pain, and I'm here to say that it's worth the wait!

NOTE

1. Martin De Haan, "Waiting in Line," *Times of Discovery* (Grand Rapids, Mich.: Radio Bible Class), December 1992, p. 2.

CHAPTER ONE

Choose to Wait with a New Attitude

"Welcome aboard Flight 703, departing Orange County to San Jose." The attendant's words barely registered as I stared at the back of the seat in front of me. My three-year-old daughter was strapped tightly next to me, and I held my six-month-old son against me.

I must be dreaming, I thought as I slumped in my seat. I hadn't slept for thirty-six hours. *Why won't my eyes shut?* As I squeezed them, the pressure of my swollen lids reminded me of the frequent outbursts of tears over the past few weeks. I was smothered by despair. My body ached, my head throbbed, and I fought nausea.

This isn't happening. . . . What will my parents think when I tell them my husband needed a little time to himself? I knew the truth. He wasn't happy in our marriage and needed distance rather than confrontation to decide its value.

As I gazed out the window, fresh tears blurred the runway lights. I felt a tugging on my sleeve. "Why do we have to wear seat belts?" my daughter questioned. "Can I have a drink of water? When will the plane go?"

Turning my head, I studied her innocent smile. *What had she said . . . seat belts . . . a drink . . . plane?*

I shook my head. "Not now, honey."

The pressures of the past few years have just caught up with him. It's only a phase. After some time he'll work it out. The best thing I can do is give him a week free from the demands of the children.

The plane's engine brought another tug on my sleeve. "Are we going, Mama?"

"Yes, honey, soon."

I'm sure being in the house alone will show him how much he wants and needs his family. When I return home, we'll start a new life together.

A flight attendant broke into my wistful reflections: "You may want to give your baby something to suck on when we take off." Mechanically, I pulled a bottle of juice from my bag and slipped it in my son's mouth.

The engine roared louder as the plane gained momentum. My baby sucked his bottle desperately. My daughter squeezed my limp hand and grinned with excitement. I forced a smile for her.

As the plane took flight, I was flooded with fear. *Someone is missing! Where is my husband?* I felt like standing in the aisle and screaming, "Help! I'm all alone!" No one on the plane knew my pain; no one understood. My eyes burned as I felt tears slip down my cheeks. I turned my head, whisking them away with the back of my sleeve. I couldn't let my children see their mom falling apart.

"Look at the lights, Mommy!"

I muttered, "Oh, pretty."

"Let's sing a song, Mommy," my daughter begged. In a joyful high-pitched voice, she began, "Jesus loves me, this I know, for the Bible tells me so."

As if they were stones, I began throwing words at God: "You love me, huh? You've caused me to hurt like this. . . . Is that love? What about this morning?"

The scene played repeatedly in my mind. After working all night as a nurse, I arrived home at 7:00 A.M. greeted by my husband's announcement, "I can't watch the children today while you sleep." He stared at the floor, looking more than his thirty years. "I don't have the patience to care for them. I need to leave the house . . . go somewhere, anywhere."

My heart raced and my voice trembled as I offered, "What would you think if I took the children to my parents for a week or so? It might give you the time and space you need to sort things out."

"I think that's a good idea. I know the children will be happier there than seeing me like this. I'd like to talk to our pastor, and maybe it would be better if I spoke to him alone." Quickly, he kissed the children good-bye and left.

Had I been abandoned only this morning? The past few weeks my husband had grown very distant. Something lay between us, but it remained a complete mystery to me. Day after day of rejection brought confusion, despair, and sleeplessness. Dropping my head back, I realized, for the first time in almost nine years, I didn't know where my husband was. He didn't know if I had actually gone to my parents. *Did he even care?*

"Aren't airplanes fun, Mommy?"

"Oh, yes, honey."

Surely, he would call my parents' house when he found us gone. He'd want to know if we had arrived safely.

"Let's sing again, Mommy!"

Anything to pass the time and keep the children happy.

I joined in, "Yes, Jesus loves me. Yes, Jesus loves me. Yes, Jesus loves me. The Bible tells me so."

Had an hour passed? The flight attendant again suggested, "You may want to give your baby something to suck on. We're getting ready to land." I pulled out a second bottle, buckled in my daughter, and held my baby tightly. Suddenly, I felt a weight of responsibility I'd never known. *I'm all alone! I'll have to make every decision by myself. He won't even be at the airport to help me carry the suitcases.*

During the thirty-minute drive to my parents' house, little was said; but after settling the children in bed, I knew my parents deserved some explanation. "Mom, I don't really know why I'm here. I'm so tired. I can't talk, think, or explain anything until I get some sleep. Can we talk in the morning?"

Despite my words, I remained rooted to the floor. Mom sank into her chair; her eyes filled with tears. My dad came over and hugged me tightly. We sobbed together. I couldn't remember another time when my dad had displayed such deep emotion.

Even after I settled down in my old room, I couldn't sleep. I kept struggling to figure things out. My husband's actions were so unlike those of the man with whom I had spent half my life. I struggled to beat off the fears that overwhelmed me. *What was to become of my future? Our future? Our children? Our home? Our jobs? Was my whole world falling apart?*

I shook my fist at the ceiling and reminded God of the injustice of my situation, reminded Him that He promised to be there when everyone else vanished. Though I didn't feel any love at that moment, I did remember a verse that said, "I will never leave you nor forsake you" (Heb. 13:5). *Maybe this was the time to take God at His word. Could I* commit my life to something I could not feel? Could I believe God's love would be so trustworthy that He would stand with me, no matter what happened in my life?

I sobbed, "Oh, God, whatever You want from me, You've got it. I need Your help! Help me sleep, think, care for my kids, make the right choices . . . follow You. I have nothing to offer You . . . except me. I feel so weak, scared, unsure, rejected, unloved. Go ahead and take me, Lord. It seems no one else wants me anyway."

The phone never rang. My pillow was drenched, but I drifted off to sleep, a solid sleep where I dreamed of waking with an unshakable faith to call my own.

IT'S CALLED WAITING TIME

I soon discovered it would take waiting time to see my dream become reality. How could I begin to see beyond my suffering? I needed to develop an attitude that could see a purpose in my pain because I knew that pain and suffering without a sense of purpose would lead me to despair and hopelessness.

You may have been separated from your spouse by no choice of your own. You may have felt like a victim when you awakened one day to the startling news, "I don't love you anymore; our marriage is over." Without warning, or even any knowledge that problems existed, you found yourself left alone to face the failure of your marriage. The grief you feel is almost unbearable.

On the other hand, perhaps for some time you have lived with an abusive mate, dealt with addiction, or had an unfaithful spouse. To be separated from your partner, due to these circumstances, has brought instant relief, not grief. As one acquaintance put it, "To everyone else, he seems like a nice guy. He goes to church, cares about our daughter, and puts up a good front. The truth is that he is rude, disrespectful, cruel, and physically abusive at home. I couldn't wait any longer. Separation has been a relief. He continues to criticize everything I do, but at least now he is only emotionally abusive. I don't have bruises on my body anymore."

In a marriage relationship, emotional disintegration and spiritual disintegration actually begin the moment one person chooses to cease honoring the commitment. The other party may or may not be aware of this decision. Physical separation may follow the rupture quickly, as it did for me, or it may come after years of dishonor. Gary Chapman in his book *Hope for the Separated* says, "Separation removes you from some of the constant pressure of conflict. It permits self-examination in which emotions can be separated from behavior. In short, it places you in an arena where you can develop a new understanding of yourself and your spouse."[1] This new understanding may or may not lead to reconciliation. I was cautioned in a session with our pastor that physical separation usually is a step toward dissolving a marriage relationship, not repairing it.

Regardless of the reasons for your separation, one fact is universal: You are *waiting*. You may be the one who filed for divorce, and you are *waiting* through the legal process: The state says you will wait four to six months for your divorce to be final. You may be *waiting* for your spouse to decide whether or when to file for divorce. You may be of the Catholic faith, legally divorced by the state, yet you are *waiting* and praying for a church annulment. You may not be considering divorce at all, but you need a separation to see your spouse from a different perspective: You are *waiting* to see if you can work things out.

Until my separation, I had never walked through such

pain or waited for anything so desperately. During your separation, waiting is not a choice. It is a given. As you wait you can, however, choose your attitude:

> *Although waiting can seem inactive and wasteful it actually accelerates our opportunity to focus on what is most important in life—to choose our attitude no matter what those in front of us are doing or not doing to make life miserable. Victor Frankl learned the high "activity" of waiting in an extreme and terrible classroom. As a survivor of holocaust concentration camps, he writes, "Everything can be taken from a man but one thing: the last of human freedoms—to choose one's attitude in any given set of circumstances."[2]*

I HATE TO WAIT!

We are all familiar with waiting; it's a fact of living. We wait for a bus to arrive, a car to be repaired, a prescription to be filled, someone to return a phone call, the mail to come. These ordinary waiting experiences are relatively easy to cope with if we know how long they will take—or until something happens to turn them into anxious waiting experiences. The bus is late after you've been told, "If you're late again, you could lose your job." The pharmacist is nowhere to be found, and your child is crying, "Mommy, I can't stand it anymore. My ear hurts so bad!" Your letter carrier arrives with an envelope: "Please sign here." He's just delivered the papers to begin your divorce proceedings.

Waiting is a lost skill in our culture. We have such poor attitudes while waiting because we aren't taught how to wait. Everything we read, hear, and watch on TV encourages instant gratification: instant food, instant tellers, instant photos, instant fax messages, instant pain relief.

When we take the quick way rather than wait, we end up settling for less and missing opportunities. We rob ourselves of growth and learning.

During my separation, as the days grew from weeks into months, I lived with never-ending uncertainty about my future. I compared my feelings with those of a patient of mine who had been diagnosed with a tumor and was waiting to hear the results from the pathologist. A benign report (representing reconciliation) would mean a change in her lifestyle for six weeks and a future essentially unchanged. A malignant report (representing divorce) could mean death. Both reports would mean surgery, leaving a scar that would remind her forever of the painful surgery she had once endured. I, too, was waiting for the report. No matter what the results, my separation would scar me for the rest of my life. Could I bear to know the results? How long could I wait?

Waiting through marital separation demands your full attention. There will be times of great confusion because you don't know what to expect. At times you will have little or no control over your situation. "To live is to wait. To wait is to suffer and rejoice, to nearly dance with delight and nearly break down with grief, . . . not because of realities that we experience but in anticipation of realities that lie ahead."[3] When you choose to acknowledge the possibility of purpose behind the pain of your separation, you are ready to grow and change. Only you can choose the attitude you want to have toward God, yourself, and your spouse as you wait.

WHAT IS MY ATTITUDE TOWARD GOD?

You can be sure your relationship with God will change as a result of your separation, for the better or for the worse. You will be closer and more intimate with God, or you will be distanced from Him. Rather than place this issue of separation between you and God, determine to involve Him in it. Your helplessness will force you to examine your attitude toward God and ask, Is He a God who causes my pain because He enjoys watching me suffer, or is He a God who allows pain because He knows there is a purpose in it?

Until my separation, many blinders conveniently allowed me to dismiss God and His desires for me. Against my will, those blinders were removed. At first it was hard to believe God could ever bring good out of the tragedy of my broken marriage. My suffering forced me to look inward and then upward to a hope and purpose beyond what the world could ever offer. I've come to experience joy—not in the absence of suffering but in the presence of God. God wanted me to know Him not only for what He could *do* for me but for who He wanted to *be* for me.

WHAT IS MY ATTITUDE TOWARD MYSELF?

My son was learning a lot in kindergarten. He was amazed to discover that tadpoles and caterpillars had something in common—they both change. One day he came running into the house with cupped hands. "Look," he said to his sister. "I caught a little frog." He opened his hands slowly and whispered, "Someday soon it will change into a butterfly!"

He remembered that the tadpole and the caterpillar had the potential to change. They were created to be different, yet they were created to change. So are we. A new attitude toward God isn't the only change that will come from your separation. You will also have a new attitude toward your-self: Should I take this opportunity to grow and change, to become new? Or should I resist and fight to stay as I am? Can I believe God's statement, "If anyone is in Christ, he is a new creation; old things have passed away; behold, all things have become new"(2 Cor. 5:17)? You can ask God's assistance to become all that He intended, or you can attempt within your own resources to become whosoever *you* desire. My new attitude about myself helped me to wait, encouraging me to seek out who I was in Christ.

As I made my bed one day, I glanced at the recently repainted bed frame. I remembered the way it once had looked. It had been darkly stained with layers of shiny varnish that reflected years of use and abuse. I remembered how much work it took to prepare the frame for repaint-ing. I used a brush and applied a very toxic varnish remover. I tried to hose off the bubbled varnish, but the chemical lifted the varnish, mixed with the water, and made a gooey mess in the hot sun. I moved the frame to the shade and applied three more coats of remover. Then I used a wire brush and all the muscle I could muster to finally strip the wood. Days later I painted coat after coat (even on the back of the frame that no one would ever see). I wanted my "new" bed frame to have no resem-blance to the scratched, dark piece it had been.

As I admired my beautiful white frame, accented in blue, I thought of the refinishing business that God is in. He had taken my life and stripped me clean when I had least expected it. The chemical (my separation) that He was using on me seemed harsh, but He promised me a beautiful new look. My God-given frame (body) would remain the same—for the time being—but my spiritual nature was brand-new. I thought of the effort it took me to make my bed frame look new. What a job God had ahead of Him to bring my thoughts and actions into line with my new nature.

It's not so much the circumstances God wants to change for us but our attitudes. I had asked God to change my marriage. Never before had I asked God to change *me*. How foolish I had been! He wanted me to know Him not only for what He could *be* for me but for what He could *make* of me. I agree with what Ben Patterson wrote in his book *Waiting:* "At least as important as the things we wait for is the work God wants to do in us as we wait."[4]

WHAT IS MY ATTITUDE TOWARD MY SPOUSE?

Your relationship with God will change as a result of your separation; you will change; and your relationship with your spouse will obviously change, too. The physical separation from your spouse will force you to examine your attitude toward your spouse. Ask yourself, Do I believe that my spouse has the potential to change? Can you believe that since God wants to (and can) remake you, He can do the same for your spouse? Can you believe that He "created man in His own image; . . . male and female He created them" (Gen. 1:27)?

All my married life I unknowingly had tried to remake my husband into my image rather than allow God to remake him into His image. I wanted to accept him as he was, but I couldn't help noticing ways he could improve. I was always eager to share my suggestions. Could I relinquish to the Lord my desire to control my husband? It was hard to believe anything good could come out of being physically separated from my husband, yet God used the time to teach me to view my husband from a different perspective: His perspective. My new attitude about my husband helped me to wait, encouraging me all the while to seek out what he could be in Christ.

My husband desired little communication during our separation, so I often shared my thoughts with him in writing:

> I've thought a lot about marriage and what it means to me. . . . I know now that only God can change me to become the right person for you. For the first time I'm willing to release you from my expectations so that we might become the right people for one another. . . .
>
> I want to offer you time and listening ears, and an open heart that comes with questions and anxieties about sharing a future with you. I realize just because I'm waiting for you, there is no guarantee of a future together. I'm willing to wait for God's next move in our lives, not my "brilliant plan."

As you read this, you might be saying, "You don't know my spouse. . . . It would take a miracle for a change to occur!" That is exactly what I'm suggesting. Only God in His sovereignty can take a situation that is impossible and make a change: "With men this is impossible, but with God all things are possible" (Matt. 19:26). Can you run the risk of being vulnerable while asking yourself and your spouse some deep, heart-wrenching questions? Just because you choose to examine yourself doesn't mean your spouse will do a self-examination. Regardless of whether or not you and your spouse are reconciled, don't miss this valuable opportunity to explore what went wrong and the potential for change. Resist the urge to push unsolved issues aside. Your new attitude must include the boldness to see potential and believe in change, and the humility to accept your spouse's free will and God's ultimate purpose. My new attitude helped me see that God wanted me to know Him not only for what He could *make* of me but for what He could *make* of my husband—in or out of our marriage.

Your pain identifies you—your choices will direct you. There is pain in anxious waiting. You can mask the pain or allow it to transform you. New attitudes toward God, yourself, and your spouse can make your wait the opportunity for growth and change. Become a frog or a butterfly; allow your spouse to grow; see your dream of unshakable faith become reality. Separation is an arena in which your choices can count not only for the day but also for eternity.

> *Dear Lord, strip my mind and heart of pain and confusion for the moment. Allow me to see nothing but You— Your love, care, strength, and power. Help me rest in Your arms for comfort and grab firmly to Your hand for guidance. Give me hope, and let me see Your purpose in my pain and suffering. Help me choose the right attitudes that will allow me to wait on You. In Jesus' name, Amen.*

WHILE YOU'RE WAITING, TAKE TIME TO CONSIDER . . .

1. What was your initial reaction to your separation? Were you surprised? Relieved? Afraid?
2. Describe a time in the past you have anxiously waited. Did the anxiety accomplish anything?
3. What makes waiting hard for you?
4. What are you expecting now? Why?
5. Who are you waiting for? Why?

6. Have you been ignoring God? Do you think He is worth getting to know better?

7. Do you think you are worth changing? What will it take for you to change?

8. Do you believe God can remake you? Your spouse? Will you let Him?

9. How are you communicating with your spouse right now?

10. Are you willing to risk being vulnerable with your spouse? Can you accept rejection?

11. Do you value free choice?

12. Can you see any purpose in your separation? In waiting?

NOTES

1. Gary Chapman, *Hope for the Separated* (Chicago: Moody Press, 1982), p. 17.

2. Martin De Haan, "Waiting in Line," *Times of Discovery* (Grand Rapids, Mich.: Radio Bible Class), December 1992, pp. 1–2.

3. Mark A. Noll, "The Agony and Ecstasy of Waiting," *Christianity Today*, November 23, 1992, p. 11.

4. Ben Patterson, *Waiting: Finding Hope When God Seems Silent* (Downers Grove, Ill.: InterVarsity Press, 1989), p. 11.

CHAPTER TWO

Choose to Learn

"How are things going? . . . I mean . . . really?" Joyce asked.

I had invited my friend over for coffee and some much-needed adult conversation. After drawing a deep breath, I asked in a soft voice, "Have you ever had so many sleepless nights you feel nauseated all the time? I can't stop crying. I got up at three this morning to change my pillowcase because I couldn't find a dry spot on it. My mind won't stop. It's as if I hear a recording of conversations and see years of memories on a video screen that I can't turn off."

"I never have trouble sleeping," Joyce responded, "except for the nights before Christmas when I lie in bed trying to think of something to get for my father-in-law. Is it like that?"

I paused to wipe away yet another trickle of tears with the back of my sleeve. "I've never been through anything like this before. I have so many questions."

"Just like our neighbor Joe, I bet. Yesterday he asked me when we were going to replace the old fence. I had to tell him, 'I just don't know. We haven't talked it over yet, but we'll let you know tomorrow.' "

Was she hearing a thing I was saying? I picked up my coffee cup with both hands to steady it. "You don't get it. I'm not talking fences here. I'm asking questions like 'Will we *ever* be able to work this out?' We can't just talk it over and have an answer tomorrow. I'm asking questions that will affect the future of lives, not backyards.

"I don't know what it will take to get through all this, but I do know I don't want to do something stupid. I'm so angry at times, I'm afraid of what I might do. Sometimes I stack up pillows on my bed and then hit them until I'm exhausted."

"Well, I know what you mean." Joyce rolled her eyes upward as she drew in a deep breath. "I was so mad last week when I started to make a casserole for dinner. I opened the refrigerator to get the cottage cheese for the recipe and discovered Gary had eaten it for lunch. It made me furious." Coffee slopped into the saucer from her shaking cup. "I had to go to the store again just to get dinner on the table."

I measured my words carefully. "I don't know when I'll ever share a meal with a man again. You have someone to cook for, and you look forward to Gary coming home at night. You have someone to share your life with . . . and you're making a case over cottage cheese!"

Joyce blushed. "I'm so sorry, Jan! I have no idea what it must be like." In a quiet, sincere voice she asked, "Why do you think your husband really left? Could he be having an affair?"

"I've always trusted him. I never had a reason *not* to. I asked him if there was anyone else. He said, 'No, I would never hurt you that way.' I guess I believe him." After a moment of silence, I admitted, "I've never known anyone who's had an affair. Do you think I shouldn't believe him?"

"I really don't know. I just asked."

"I always thought I was a good wife and mother. I never

thought of myself as such a loser or so unlovable. Do you think I'm a good person?"

"Of course you are. You're my best friend."

"Then why would God punish me like this? Why is this happening to me? I thought if I just prayed hard enough, we'd face this head-on and make a new life together. Isn't that what God would want?"

"Well, I'm sure He wants the best for you."

"Oh, Joyce, I'm so afraid. I shouldn't be afraid if I'm a Christian, should I?"

Joyce hugged me tightly as I wept. It felt good just to be held.

"What exactly are you afraid of?"

"I'm afraid of illness," I admitted.

"We all get sick. Is that really something to be afraid of?"

"It's different now that I feel the children are dependent on me. If I got sick and was out of work just two days, I couldn't make the house payment. What will happen now if *they* get sick? I can't take time off work to be with them, and I'll never have enough money to take them to a doctor.

"I'm afraid for their safety, too. Last night I got up three times to make sure all the doors and windows were locked. What if someone broke in and something happened?

"Maybe all of this will be like last year when my wallet was stolen. At first I felt so violated, and I wondered if I'd ever get it back. I waited and then replaced the contents. After that, it didn't seem to matter to me if I ever got it back. Do you think losing my marriage will be like that?"

"No, Jan. I think you've been telling me that your marriage has far more meaning than a driver's license and some credit cards. You can't toss it out, replace it, and never think of it again."

WHY SHOULD I TRY TO LEARN AND UNDERSTAND?

As I shared my feelings with Joyce, she helped me see I had spent most of my life focused on Christmas presents, fences, and cottage cheese. My separation forced me to see life from a different perspective. I realized, whether I liked it or not, I had a lot to learn. I needed to find some answers to my unending questions: Is being filled with anger and fear normal? Will I always feel so alone and such a failure? Are these feelings a result of my situation, or are they an accurate reflection of me as a person? How will I talk to other people about my separation?

Choose to learn while you wait. It can mean the difference between living successfully in the future or continuing to feel your life has been a failure. Choosing to learn moves you from a place of stagnation into the arena of growth. You might be saying, as I once did, "If learning means going through an arduous self-examination, I'd rather keep my eye out for an easier solution. Maybe I will find contentment in my ignorance." However, your separation is a fact. You are a student in this class whether you like it or not. It is your choice to pass or fail, learn or remain ignorant. Your feelings about separation and your ongoing reactions can be the problem or the solution. As you learn, you will begin to fight for the life of your marriage or begin to accept its death.

WHY AM I SEPARATED?

Judeo-Christian values were once reinforced by almost every social structure in our society: jobs, schools, neighbors, churches, television, and movies. The divorce statistics of our day reflect the shift from traditional family values and the acceptance of divorce as a viable alternative to marriage.

Despite the emotional and financial difficulties, about 80 percent of those who have been divorced are willing to remarry.[1] One writer observed, "Divorce has overtaken widowhood as the leading cause of marital dissolution and in a rising proportion of American couples at least one partner has been married and divorced before entering their current marriage."[2] According to the Stepfamily Association of America, every third marriage is a remarriage for at least one of the partners.[3]

With divorce and remarriage so prevalent, separation may be familiar to you because you've walked through the experience with family and friends. But personally, it may be unfamiliar. Your preconceptions regarding someone who is separated will now be validated or shattered by your experience. You will see many common denominators as well as unique differences. Remember, each separation has its own story: the past lives of two unique individuals and their present interactions with children, relatives, and friends. I will be sharing information based on my studies and my experiences. You will need to take your situation into consideration as you apply this information.

You still may be scratching your head and asking, "Why did this ever happen to us?" Or you may have seen the breakdown of your relationship coming for years. It has been said that there is no 100 percent innocent party. Just as it takes two people to make a successful marriage, so it takes two people to cause its breakdown. You may be saying, "You've obviously never seen a situation like mine. I'm not at fault. I had every right to walk out on this one!" You may be correct; however, marriage is a relationship with a person, not a relationship with a situation.

From my studies, I have learned that most relationships

break down because one partner can no longer cope with a situation that both partners are responsible for creating. It's important for both partners to have the willingness and capacity to take responsibility for what went wrong. If you examine your relationship and discover the reasons for the failure, you will be in a better position to make the necessary changes after a reconciliation or later on in a different relationship. Rather than point a finger, take this time to analyze the part you may have played in the deterioration of your relationship. Moving past the blame game marks you as a student ready for growth and change.

Joyce's questions about my husband led me to examine the real reasons for his leaving. I learned that couples give marriage counselors a million reasons for their decision to separate and eventually divorce. However, according to Jim Smoke in his book *Growing Through Divorce*, there are seven basic situational causes that occur repeatedly.[4] You probably will identify with one of them.

1. The "Victim" Separation

One person usually wants the separation while the other person does not. Often one mate leaves the home for another lover. The departure may have come suddenly without warning. However, it is also possible to have ignored for a long time the obvious hints of an unhappy spouse, hoping the problems would just disappear. The mate left behind often is first merely surprised, then truly shocked, and feels rejection, guilt, worthlessness, and despair. These feelings often turn into anger and revenge. The mate who leaves may be confused but has a sense of confidence in a new relationship and/or direction. If you are looking for information on extramarital affairs, I suggest you read *The Myth of the Greener Grass* by J. Allan Petersen. He speaks frankly and provides both preventive and healing measures. *The Prodigal Spouse* by Dr. Les Carter is another excellent resource.

2. The "Problem" Separation

One or both partners have a destructive and/or obsessive "problem." The problem may involve physical or emotional abuse. It may involve addictions to alcohol, gambling, drugs, or pornography. There may have been numerous affairs, lies, and cover-ups. The enabling spouse who in the past had protected the addict from the consequences of the abuse may have said finally, "I just won't. . . . I can't take it anymore!" If this is your situation, you may vacillate from feelings of sympathy for your spouse to feelings of regret that you tolerated the behavior for so long. If you are the spouse with the problem, you may feel anger and hostility for being abandoned, and you may feel powerless to change enough to make things right.

Whether or not you are the one with the problem, take time to study the specific problem, such as drugs or alcohol. Discover how it can affect you, your spouse, and your family. Perhaps you know you have disabled your spouse by being an enabler. A book such as *Love Is a Choice* by Robert Hemfelt, Frank Minirth, and Paul Meier or *Love Must Be Tough* by James Dobson will help you gain the necessary insight to risk breaking the cycle.

3. The "Little Boy, Little Girl" Separation

This separation involves one mate who no longer wants the responsibility of being a spouse or parent. The individual wants to spend time with "the girls" (or "the boys") and play with the "toys" enjoyed before marriage. The one left behind feels rejected while the other often has no sense of remorse.

4. The "I Was Conned" Separation

This separation comes when one mate fails to get what was expected from the marriage. The dishonesty of one person can lead to disillusionment. At other times one mate simply wakes up from a self-created fantasy. The one who stays behind likely feels defensive. The one who leaves feels justified and confident, believing it necessary to "move on with life."

5. The "Shotgun" Separation

I'm sure you've heard of the "shotgun" wedding for the pregnant bride. Family and friends feel it is the honorable way to resolve the problem. Pressure in this kind of marriage by necessity is often too great. Both bride and groom feel "under the gun" to prove to themselves and to others that it will work out (even if they questioned it themselves from the start). Both parties may have feelings that run from pity to rejection.

6. The "Menopause or Midlife" Separation

Dramatic changes in personality and behavior can cause either husband or wife to want to leave the other. Because these changes usually take place after many years of marriage, there are confusion, deep hurt and bitterness, and feelings of abandonment. The feelings described in the victim separation are very similar to those in a midlife separation. There are predictable problems facing both men and women in midlife. You and your partner will gain understanding of these specific problems from *Men in Mid-Life Crisis* by Jim Conway and *You and Your Husband's Mid-Life Crisis* by Sally Conway. Both can gain insight into a woman's midlife struggle by reading *Emotional Phases of a Woman's Life* by Jean Lush.

7. The "No Fault" Separation

Two people agree they have "had it" with each other. They decide together that things will never work out, and they go their separate ways. It's possible in this situation to feel very neutral toward each other, having no desire to fault the other because the separation was a mutual agreement.

Did you identify with one of the common problems described in the illustrations? If not, many resources present other explanations for separation. For instance, Bob Burns in *Recovery from Divorce* discusses the breakdown of friendship, trust, communication, shared goals, and marital intimacy.[5] Perhaps you can identify more easily with these relational reasons for your separation rather than with the situational ones I previously mentioned. All these explanations are broad generalizations, but our marriages do share many common problems. Although your marriage is unique, it is helpful to remember that we can learn from one another.

HOW WILL I FEEL, AND WHO CAN I TELL?

"I'm so upset with myself," Joan told me. "I just had a conversation on the phone with my husband. I was so angry, and nothing came out the way I meant it to. I'm so embarrassed. I just had to talk to someone who understands."

It is likely that you are living through something you have never experienced before. Often your emotions will seem out of control (even after you have gained new insights about the best way to handle a situation). You may think, *The next time I see her I will smile and quietly tell her* _____ (you fill in the blank). The time comes. You see her. Your emotions take over, and you act in a manner you never thought possible.

Your anger, fears, and desires don't make you a good or bad person: "Emotions are not moral but simply factual."[6] However, what you choose to do with your feelings does involve morality; the actions you take based on your feelings can be right or wrong. You will experience a multitude of natural, normal emotions that range from fear and anger to hate, grief, and even bitterness. The more you learn about what feelings to expect, the better prepared you will be to respond appropriately to others. You will be free from the guilt that may result from well-intended remarks such as, "You shouldn't feel that way!" The Bible offers us hope when it reminds us in Ecclesiastes 3:1–8 that "to everything there is a season": a time to love, and a time to hate. Choose an appropriate time and place to express your feelings.

You need to know how to be selective when you choose someone to confide in. You may be able to share your honest feelings safely with relatives, church friends, pastor, neighbors, or other supportive friends. Share how you are feeling at the moment, even though your feelings will change (perhaps within the hour). Sometimes you need to share aloud to clarify your thoughts. True friends will allow you to vent your feelings. Though Joyce didn't always understand how I felt, she helped me to identify my feelings with her feedback.

Remember you are presenting the situation of your separation from your perspective. It will be natural for family and friends to react to the details and align themselves either with you or with your spouse. Your job is to be as factual and honest as possible. Allow others to come to their own conclusions. As you share your feelings, be careful you don't burn your bridges during a time when you may be unsure of your motives. Don't play the blame game and point a finger at someone else. There are family relationships with grandparents, brothers, sisters, aunts; uncles, and cousins that you and your spouse will want to preserve, no matter what the outcome of your separation. If you try to get more on your side by assassinating your spouse's character, you may create tension in a relationship that both of you need for love and support, now and in the future.

There should be nothing but honesty between you and your children regarding your separation. Honesty builds trust. It's not necessary, or even wise, to share *everything* with young children, though. How can you expect them to have the maturity to cope with a situation that you don't understand yourself? Your job is to allow them to be children. Provide them freedom to express their feelings, but don't burden them with yours. Respond to their feelings and questions on their level. Tell them the truth, but only what is necessary to answer their specific questions. Details are seldom required; however, it is unfair not to prepare them for comments they may receive from their peers or even well-meaning adults.

Steve was afraid to tell his junior high daughter the real reason for her mother's departure. "Julie, you know Mom finds it hard to stay home all day taking care of the house. She needed to get away for a while, so she took a trip with the Fosters. Maybe after a little vacation, things will be OK." There were some truths in that story. Julie's mom did find it hard to stay at home, and due to her addiction to drugs and alcohol, she often took "trips." In a state of depression she ran off to the Fosters, new friends she had met at Alcoholics Anonymous. The untold truth was that several months ago Mr. Foster's wife had left. Julie's mom was having an affair with Mr. Foster.

Bryan, a kid in Mr. Foster's neighborhood, had noticed an extra car parked in Mr. Foster's driveway for over a week. He realized the car belonged to Julie's mom after he saw her kissing Mr. Foster good-bye in the driveway. Bryan approached Julie at school and said, "So what's with your mom and Mr. Foster, huh?" Julie was unprepared. She thought Mom would be home soon after "a little vacation" with the Foster family, and "things would be OK."

Every circumstance is different. Take into consideration your children's maturity level, and prepare them for the truth in a timely fashion. My children, for instance, were so young they didn't know what the word *affair* meant. At first it wasn't necessary to tell them all the facts relating to their father's departure. As they got older and began spending the night at their dad's house, they needed more facts: "It makes God very sad that Mommy and Daddy aren't living together anymore. It makes Mommy sad, too. Daddy says he doesn't love Mommy anymore. He loves Helen now, the way he used to love Mommy. That's why you may see them kissing each other or hugging." That information was all they needed for a time.

When they began putting the pieces together for themselves, I tried to answer their questions as honestly as I could. "Since Daddy loves Helen now, does that mean he won't ever live with us anymore?" my four-year-old asked. "It is possible Daddy will never live here again. Daddy is very mixed up right now, and so am I. It's going to take time to see what will happen," I replied.

Above all, in this time of uncertainty your children don't need the added pressure of being forced to take sides. *Listen to what your children are saying,* and help them put their feelings into words. It is not easy to create an environment where they feel safe enough to share their feelings. It must be a conscious part of your daily interaction with them.

You will relate to adult children on an entirely different level. They, too, need to sort through their feelings regarding your separation. Though your children are grown, they need to be granted the privilege of remaining your children, not your confidants and counselors.

Face your separation head-on by admitting to yourself, to others, and to God how you feel. Then you will be free to become an honest person: acknowledging your humanity by admitting your mistakes, and then learning from them. Much of this book is intended to help you learn about the emotions you can expect during your separation and discover healthy ways to express them. This may be the time to seek out a professional counselor to guide you in discovering your feelings. You may need help to overcome depression and/or gain a proper perspective of your situation. I'll talk about counseling in the next chapter. Having an honest understanding of yourself will help you develop the responsible attitudes and actions you need while you wait.

WHAT DOES GOD THINK ABOUT SEPARATION?

"Will I ever get over the guilt I have?" Bob asked. "I'm a Christian, and I'm the one who asked my wife to leave. I just couldn't take it anymore. Does that mean I have disobeyed God?"

My intention is not to judge whether or not you are justified in your present separation or possible divorce. My desire is to recommend resources so you may better understand God's design for marriage. One day you will want to stand with complete confidence before a holy God knowing that you have obeyed Him, divorced or not.

I believe without a doubt that God has the highest regard for life, marriage, and the family unit. These are among His creations. He is the One who created the union of man and woman for companionship, joy, nurturing, and procreation. To reject marriage is to reject one of God's designs. Does this mean, however, that all marriages are considered holy, as He designed them to be, and that *all* Scriptures regarding marriage and divorce can be applied to *every* marriage? I gained a new understanding of Scripture as I read M. G. McLuhan's book *Marriage and Divorce: God's Call, God's Compassion*. I recommend it to you. Spiros Zodhiates also has written a helpful book, *May I Divorce and Remarry?* In commentary fashion it answers in great detail many questions about God's view of separation and divorce.

God intends marriage to be not only a physical oneness but also an emotional and spiritual union that glorifies Him. If both parties are operating perfectly as Spirit-filled and Spirit-led individuals, *nothing* should be able to separate them. I am confident in making that statement because we, as Christians, are the only people on earth who possess a power greater than ourselves, God Himself. He promises to work in us through His Holy Spirit, to make us like Himself. To that end, "all things are possible to him [and her] who believes" (Mark 9:23).

There is no question in my mind that the separation of two Spirit-filled and Spirit-led Christians calls for reconciliation. Two Christians should not give up on their marriage until much prayer, counseling, and genuine effort have been devoted to reconciling their relationship. Here's the good news. God won't leave you alone to face the dilemma. He promises His Holy Spirit to guide you to all truth (John 16:13–14), convict you of sin (John 16:8–11), comfort you (John 14:16), and produce fruits within you (Gal. 5:22–23). Gary Chapman's *Hope for the Separated* and Jim Talley's *Reconcilable Differences* are excellent resources. They provide instruction and hope; reconciliation is possible and attainable following recommended guidelines. Jim and Sally Conway also discuss how to go about saving your marriage based on proven counseling techniques in their book *When One Mate Wants Out*.

Although God's desire is for reconciliation, none of us walk perfectly in this life, Christians or not. In *The Fresh Start Divorce Recovery Workbook*, Bob Burns and Tom Whiteman suggest five essential elements necessary for reconciliation. It takes (1) two people, (2) an honest evaluation of past problems and personal mistakes, (3) mutual repentance and forgiveness, (4) rebuilding of trust, and (5) time and effort.[7]

God Himself said that He hates divorce (Mal. 2:16). It is a rip in the fabric of His design for His creation. I believe, just as He desires that all come to a saving knowledge of Himself, He also desires that all marriages be a duet, not a solo: two people giving themselves unreservedly to each other (Gen. 2:25). However, God offers us a choice: to accept Him and His blueprint for living, or to reject Him. Just as God doesn't force you to love Him, neither can you force your spouse to love you. It must be an act of the will. You may desire reconciliation, but the first criterion is "it takes two." Many times this is the most difficult requirement to accept. It was for me.

If you are wondering why you should bother to spend the effort to make things work, take time to read some words of warning in *The Divorce Decision* by Gary Richmond. He offers insights into the consequences that divorce will have for your children, your finances, your emotions, your relationships, and your future. The consequences of divorce are far-reaching and require your careful consideration.

As you allow God to convict and direct you, you will be dissatisfied with even a shred of evidence that you may be violating His will. There is no reason to run ahead of God. You will win His approval, to say nothing about peace of mind, by waiting on Him to reveal His will for you. As you seek God's instruction in the direction of your marriage through His Word, godly counsel, and prayer, the Holy Spirit *will* provide you assurance. You will receive freedom from guilt when you know you have been obedient to God.

IS THERE ANY HOPE?

Because of Mindy's sobs, I could barely hear her voice over the phone. "What good can ever come of this?" she asked. "My whole life is ruined. I have no hope."

Indeed, Mindy will continue to feel hopeless if she dwells on the causes of her separation and lives in the past instead of using her separation as an arena for growth, looking to the future. God alone is the One who truly can heal her pain, change her, and offer purpose in her life, no matter what caused her separation. Your separation is providing you this same opportunity to learn about Him. Go ahead and take it! The more you know about God, the more you will love Him. The more you love Him, the more you will be motivated to obey Him because we are all motivated to please those we love. As you learn how to get serious with God, you will have hope and an indescribable peace in the midst of the restlessness of separation.

As you begin to understand that God grieves for you, He will become approachable. He is saddened to see your emotions damaged, your children affected, your world turned upside down. When you understand that God doesn't always spare you from bad choices and calamity but does allow circumstances to humble you, your perspective of Him will change. You will appreciate your free will and a God who offers hope and forgiveness, not just a pronouncement of judgment.

I felt it was very unfair that I had little choice but to go along with my spouse's demands; you may feel the same way. Even though you can't change your spouse's decisions, you *are* responsible for your own. If you have prayed and made every effort to restore your marriage, and your spouse still refuses, where does that leave you? With your hand in the hand of God.

You may feel like my friend Debbie. Her eyes were moist, and her voice cracked as she said, "All I want is my husband to come back. I've prayed and prayed for six months. God obviously doesn't hear me." On the contrary, He does hear your prayers, and He does answer, although His answers may not come in the manner you expect. He is no less sovereign, and His promises are no less true. In fact, He makes the statement, "My thoughts are not your thoughts, nor are your ways My ways" (Isa. 55:8).

The more you learn about who God is and how He works in lives, the more your trust in Him will grow. You can start to believe He *is* working on your behalf, no matter what the future holds for your marriage.

In the book of Hebrews, we are told that Christ learned obedience through suffering (5:8). Why should we be any different? Through our sufferings, we, too, can learn to become obedient to a God who is more interested in the condition of our hearts than the condition of our marriages. Only when our hearts are yielded, responding with humility, can He bring about change in us and, ultimately, in our marriages.

Your pain identifies you—your choices will direct you. Many times we are tempted to do anything, even the wrong thing, rather than wait and commit ourselves to the task of learning. Be careful if you feel like this. You may discover there *is* something worse than waiting—wishing you had waited! Choose to learn about your situation, yourself, and God as you wait.

> *Dear Lord, help me to be honest with myself and with You. I want to see my separation from Your perspective. Help me find answers to the questions that do have immediate answers, and teach me to leave the rest of my questions in Your hands. In Jesus' name, Amen.*

WHILE YOU'RE LEARNING, TAKE TIME TO CONSIDER . . .

1. Do you have preconceived ideas about separation? Do you want them to be true?
2. Do you identify with one of the seven situational causes for separation and divorce? Which one?
3. Do you see an "innocent" and a "guilty" party in your separation?
4. Do you think it is possible for your marriage to be reconciled? Why? Why not?
5. What specific questions do you have about your separation?
6. Are you gathering troops for your side of the case? What relationships do you need to preserve? How will you do that?

7. Do your children know the truth about your separation?
8. What emotions do you have that surprise or embarrass you?
9. Who can you honestly share your feelings with?
10. What do you need to do to learn about yourself?
11. How can you learn more about God and His view of marriage?
12. What do you think is God's job in the midst of your separation? How do you think He should go about it?

NOTES

1. Sarnoff, *Love-Centered Marriage in a Self-Centered World*, p. 4.

2. Martin King Whyte, *Dating, Mating and Marriage* (New York: Aldine de Gruyter, 1990), p. 236.

3. Elizabeth Mehren, "Family Feuds," *Los Angeles Times*, September 16, 1992, p. E1.

4. Jim Smoke, *Growing Through Divorce* (Eugene, Oreg.: Harvest House, 1976), pp. 30–31.

5. Bob Burns, *Recovery from Divorce* (Nashville: Thomas Nelson, 1992), pp. 39–44.

6. John Powell, *Why Am I Afraid to Tell You Who I Am?* (Niles, Ill.: Argus Communications, 1969), p. 71.

7. Bob Burns and Tom Whiteman, *The Fresh Start Divorce Recovery Workbook* (Nashville: Oliver-Nelson, 1992), pp. 65–67.

CHAPTER THREE

Choose to Grieve

"Next please." The gray-haired store clerk smiled as she eyed the outfits draped over my arm. She began removing the price tags and said, "How cute! Sure wish I could wear this size."

"Believe it or not, it's the first time I've ever dropped two sizes in just three months."

"That's wonderful. How'd you do it?"

"It's been a cinch," I replied. "I don't have an appetite. I eat whatever I want. . . . The pounds just fall off."

"Oh, I wish I didn't want to eat. That would be great!" She began punching buttons on the cash register and then looked up, "Will that be cash or charge?"

"Check," I replied. I entered the name of the department store on my check. Suddenly, I recognized the song playing over the store speaker. Without warning, tears filled my eyes. I hoped the clerk wouldn't notice as I wiped them away.

"What's wrong? I thought you were so happy with your new clothes *and* your new size."

"Do you hear that song?" I asked. "When my husband and I met . . . that was 'our' song. We've been separated three months. I guess I lied a few minutes ago. . . . The pounds have been falling off, but it hasn't been easy. It's been the hardest time of my life."

"Honey, don't be embarrassed." She handed me a tissue. "Five years ago when I was grieving over my husband's death, I remember crying at the oddest times, too."

WHAT'S HAPPENING TO ME?

As I was driving home, I began to wonder what a woman whose husband died had in common with a woman whose marriage was dying. *Could I actually be grieving over someone who is still alive?*

I soon discovered that I was going through a very predictable process. I *was* grieving over a death, the death of a relationship. As I began to understand more about grieving, my feelings no longer seemed so out of control. I was better prepared to face what lay ahead in the normal, necessary process that leads to healing. I discovered that God uses the process of grieving to make those who suffer whole. To move from the place of pain you, too, must go *through* the grieving process; you do not simply *get over* the pain.[1] You will never get through the process and on to peace and freedom unless you choose to feel your pain and express your grief fully.

WHAT IS GRIEF?

One author states, "Grief is a universal, complex, and painful process of dealing with and adjusting to loss."[2] We experience grief when we lose someone or something we hold dear: a person, a pet, a job, a physical ability, a dream, or a vision of life. Elisabeth Kübler-Ross in her book *On Death and Dying* first popularized the stages of grief we know today as denial, anger, bargaining, depression, and acceptance. These stages are not scientific or biblical, yet they seem to shed light on the pattern or structure of grief, one of the most common human experiences. If you have concerns about using this model, I refer you to Bob Burns's book. In an appendix he discusses thoroughly "the validity of using the stages of grief model."[3]

If you progress without complication through these five stages, you can expect the grieving process to take up to two years. That doesn't mean you'll feel miserable constantly for two years. However, you may have to wait two years to experience a restored sense of emotional balance. The process might take longer if your separation drags on, unresolved for a protracted period of time, or if you get stuck in a particular stage. If you hold on to unrealistic hopes or fears, experience severe chronic depression, or are unable to forgive, it can take years to complete the grieving process.

Although grief can be defined and predictable stages identified, the grieving process is far from orderly. Not everyone will progress through these stages in the same order or in the same time frame. Looking back at her year of grief, Jean admitted, "I studied up on this grief thing, and I thought I knew just what to expect. I'd tell myself, 'Oh, look, now I'm in the anger stage, or now I'm in the bargaining stage. Now I'll be able to move on and accept this whole thing.' The next thing I'd know, I was right back at the beginning."

There'll be times you'll be "up," making great progress along the path. Then there'll be times you'll be "down," almost losing sight of the path. Remember you are on the road that will take you to a place of healing. Be patient, and don't try to rush things. As a fifty-five-year-old separated grandmother told me, "It's nice to know there is hope. To think one day I won't wake up analyzing what *went* wrong, what *is* wrong, or what *will be* wrong. I can't wait to enjoy a day without thinking too hard or too much about anything. It's hard to wait, but I won't give up!"

The paths we take to our desired destination of acceptance will vary, blazed by individual circumstances, personality, and temperament. The depth of our grief will vary; the intensity depends greatly on the quality of the relationship lost. The more time, emotion, expectation, effort, or money invested, the greater the sense of loss. Our expressions of grief also will vary, but they are surprisingly predictable. William Worden groups normal behaviors into four general categories: (1) feelings, (2) physical sensations, (3) cognitions (thought patterns), and (4) behaviors.[4]

1. Feelings

The most common is sadness, often expressed by crying. However, crying is not essential; many people are sad but dry-eyed. Anxiety is quite common as you react to your fear of the unknown. It can "range from a light sense of insecurity to a strong panic attack."[5] You may also feel lonely. (I will talk extensively about loneliness in chapter 7.) I previously mentioned that separation may bring a feeling of relief. Guilt may be felt; it might occur independently, but more often than not, it actually accompanies relief. Shock, anger, and helplessness are other predictable emotions. (For women, these emotions may be intensified by mood swings due to hormonal fluctuations.)

2. Physical Sensations

The most common are "hollowness in the stomach, tightness in the chest, tightness in the throat, and an oversensitivity to noise."[6] There can also be "a sense of depersonalization: 'I walk down the street and nothing seems real, including myself.' "[7] Other sensations include "feeling short of breath, weakness in the muscles, lack of energy, and a dry mouth."[8] Many people report gastrointestinal upsets, headaches, and backaches.

3. Thought Patterns

These patterns change with time as you go through the grieving process. Some are especially common in the early stages.[9] Disbelief is usually the first reaction. The recurring thought is: *This can't be happening; there must be some mistake.* Confusion is another early reaction, resulting in poor judgment, poor concentration, and forgetfulness.[10] Finally, there is a preoccupation with thoughts about what has been lost.

4. Behaviors

In the early stages of grief it is common to have trouble falling asleep or staying asleep. You may or may not have dreams relating to your loss, but dreams can be helpful indicators of where you are in your grieving process. Your eating habits will probably change, but both undereating and overeating are normal.[11] It is also normal to wish to be alone for a time or to cry uncontrollably.

Time usually brings all these disturbing, unexpected feelings, sensations, thoughts, and behaviors back into line. The pain might not end tomorrow, but there is an order to the process and you can get through it.

WHO GRIEVES?

The one who instigates the separation usually begins the grieving process well before the other. That person has faced the loss of love and dreams, possibly moving all the way through the grieving process, before the other is even aware that the marriage is in trouble. The one who is left behind often feels bewildered, wondering, What happened? What went wrong? Why does my spouse seem so unmoved by my pain? This difference in timing helps to explain why the one who leaves can be so dispassionate, even happy-go-lucky, while the other is so traumatized.

"I guess I grieved for years and didn't know I was going through a process," the forty-five-year-old wife of an alcoholic told me. "I remember when it hit me. I told myself, 'I can't believe it, but we have no relationship together.' After that I was mad at everything and everybody. I was angry with myself for letting things go so long, angry with my husband for his actions, angry with my kids for the demands they placed on me, angry with God for allowing it all, angry at alcohol and what it had done to my family, angry that I felt a helpless victim. I pleaded with my husband to stop drinking, and I promised to go to AA meetings with him if he'd just stop. Then I was depressed for years when I realized things would never change. I see now I went through all the stages of grief even before I left my husband. He tried to make me feel guilty for not feeling sorry when I left. What he didn't know was I had spent *years* feeling sorry about it."

Those of us who have been left behind usually face a lack of social support. There is no funeral or wake or traditional activity or pattern to follow. If our loss had been a physical death, friends would have rallied around us. They might have brought casseroles, offered to watch the children, and sent cards of sympathy. However, you probably haven't had any casseroles delivered to your door or received any cards. If your friends know you are separated (and you may not be spreading the news as quickly as you would in the case of a physical death), they feel sorry for you but have no idea how to help you.

For those who are left to grieve, there are other differences between the loss of a life and the loss of a relationship. In *A Severe Mercy*, Sheldon Vanauken comments on a letter he received from C. S. Lewis: "But the radical proposition . . . is that death might be the 'easiest and least perilous of the ways to lose one's love.' . . . Loves 'must always be lost.' "[12]

Loss of life is final. There never will be an opportunity to communicate or be in a relationship with the deceased again on this earth. You can make a clean break with your emotions. During separation, you face a final loss, yet options remain. The what-ifs create uncertainty. A man at a seminar said to me, "One day I want it to be over forever. The next, I hope we can work things out." If you have children, you continue to face the need to interact for years to come with your spouse, your lost love. "I know I'm supposed to stop loving her," my friend Bill said. "But how can I do that if I have to see her every other weekend for the next ten years?"

After a physical death, a sense of companionship can still exist through the memories of love. The loss of a relationship through alienation, however, usually brings feelings of rejection and failure. Rejection contributes to a lowered self-esteem: *There must be something wrong with me. I'm no good, and I'll never have anything good to offer anyone.*

After a physical death, love and respect for the deceased often grow. Physical death usually prompts us to "look for the good" in the one we have lost. Not so with the loss of a relationship. We often begin to "look for the bad" in the relationship we've lost. Disrespect, hatred, and bitterness result.

An additional difficulty is that as a parent (70 percent of all separated people are parents)[13] you will be working not only to move through your grief but also to help your children move through theirs. Because you are doing double duty, it might be difficult to recognize and respond appropriately to the emotional needs of your children.

Children's questions are endless, "Where is my daddy? I miss him. Do you miss him, too, Mommy? When is he coming back? Is he coming back?" I suggest the book *Innocent Victims* by Thomas Whiteman, Ph.D. It is written to help you and your children overcome the trauma of divorce. Don't let the word *divorce* scare you from this excellent resource. You and your children will face many of the same issues in separation. You will gain insights into the reactions you can expect from your children and be better prepared to meet their needs.

WHAT HAPPENS WHEN I GRIEVE?

Stage 1: Denial

Your grieving process begins when you learn that you have lost or are in the process of losing your marriage relationship. For me, it began the evening my husband announced, "I'm going to look for an apartment tomorrow. I'll move out as soon as I find something." Granted, I had known for a couple of weeks there was a possibility of losing my marriage, but his announcement verified the truth I had hoped to avoid. I was shocked and immediately went into denial.

I learned that my feelings were very typical as other friends shared similar experiences with me. "I still can't believe it," said Bill, a friend from high school. "I don't know what to do. I just can't believe a mother could walk out on her children."

"I keep thinking about his plans to leave me. . . . I just can't believe it," said another friend. "I was awake off and on all last night. I felt like I swallowed a hot coal; my insides burned like fire. Will I ever feel normal again?"

Denial is the first stage in the grieving process. The initial shock usually lasts two or three weeks. Common emotional manifestations include confusion, numbness, and uncontrollable weeping. This initial phase that buffers us from reality gives us time to prepare for what is to come. In their book, Tom Whiteman and Bob Burns share that denial protects us emotionally from the full pain of a loss, just as the shock response shields the body from the full pain of an injury. As the body begins to heal, feeling returns to the injured area. The same is true for emotional healing. Over a period of months, you will gradually become ready to face reality and your true feelings.[14]

After the initial period of shock passes, denial turns into a time of disbelief. It is possible to be separated for years and not move past this stage. You can blindly assert during your entire separation that one day you will be reconciled. Only when you find yourself divorced will you actually begin moving past this stage of grief.

Some Christians may use their religious faith to prolong denial. If they perceive a "good Christian" *only* as one whose marriage would never fail and they believe they are good Christians, of course, their marriages will not fail (even if they already have). If their perception of God is that He will *always* heal a Christian marriage, no matter what, they will wait to see God perform His miracle, whether it's been one year or ten. I've seen Christians hold on to the hope that God will *make* their ex-spouses come back, even when those mates are already remarried. Hope should be connected with realism.

Eventually, your loss will bring you face-to-face with change and uncertainty. You might be plagued with a variety of fears or with one single overwhelming fear. Norma, whose children were all under seven, asked, "How will I ever support myself and four kids?" Pam, a mother of three teenagers, had a completely different fear: "I was the victim of incest as a child. Over the past ten years I've replaced my own family with my husband's. If we get divorced, things will change; I'll have no family." Bill asked, "How can I raise girls to act the way girls are supposed to? Girls need a mom to teach them about 'girl things.' What will I do? I'm a man."

Initially, you will encounter hundreds of fears, and they will seem more than you can handle at times. It is tempting to stay in the safe, anesthetized stage of denial, holding the false perception that maybe you will never really have to face your fears and the truth about your marriage. Fear is the emotion most to blame for keeping you in denial when it's time to confront the reality of your separation. Worry feeds fears and is a normal reaction to circumstances beyond your control. Jesus said not to worry about our lives because He will take care of us (Matt. 6). If we can learn to trust Him and take Him at His word, we can stop worrying. When you go from saying, "I can't believe this is happening to me," to, "This *has* happened to me," you're ready to move on.

Stage 2: Anger

After you accept the reality of your loss, you will enter the second stage of grief: anger. You *are* separated, like it or not. Now what? Probably, you will be forced to make decisions you had never planned to make. You will be asked to alter the dreams you had for your life, your marriage, your children. "This is not how I saw my life," a frustrated sixty-five-year-old grandfather told me. "I never expected to have to live like this."

"It's just not fair," said a dapper, thirty-eight-year-old executive. "I'm working harder than I've ever worked to support my family. I've lost everything that ever mattered, and I never got a chance. It makes me so mad! I lie awake at night thinking of ways to make her pay for the hurt she's caused me."

Charles Swindoll in his excellent book *Three Steps Forward, Two Steps Back* defines *anger* as "an emotional reaction of hostility that brings personal displeasure, either to ourselves or to someone else."[15] After hearing that definition, anger doesn't sound like an emotion we should go out of our way to experience, does it? Swindoll goes on to say, however, that there is something inhuman about a person who never gets angry. Anger is a God-given emotion, not always a sin. It can be healthy, and it is sometimes necessary. It is a response to our deep fears, frustrations, and insecurities. Many Christians think they must skip this stage because *good* Christians shouldn't get angry. However, God gives us permission to be angry: "Be angry, and do not sin" (Eph. 4:26).

Our angry feelings may not be sinful, but what we choose to do with them may be. When anger goes unchecked and is used purposely to hurt others, it is sin. Your anger may be directed at God, your spouse, your children, your in-laws, your job, your pet, well-meaning friends, even yourself. During separation, anger can be selfishly used to put your spouse down, to seek revenge (no matter what the cost), and to justify your irresponsible actions.

There are four ways to deal with anger. Two are negative and two are positive.

1. *Rage*. Anger vents your emotions. Uncontrolled, anger becomes rage, often getting you into trouble. Your furniture, doors, pets, children, and spouse can receive the fury of your rage. Proverbs 14:16–17 asserts, "A fool rages and is self-confident. A quick-tempered man acts foolishly."

2. *Repression*. Rather than express your anger, in repression you hold it inside. This may sound like a good option, but it, too, can be destructive because it takes its toll on your body. Studies show repression reduces your body's ability to defend itself.

3. *Redirection*. This is one of the two better approaches. Turn your angry energy into something positive and productive. Given time, you should be able to accept, forgive, and constructively approach your mate, but until such time redirect your feelings and your energies. Take a step to make even a small improvement. Begin an exercise program, take a night class, or pursue a new hobby. Try to share your time by volunteering at school or church. There are lots of options. (Check out the list of "Survival Tips" at the end of this chapter.) You can find great satisfaction in doing something positive when everything else seems negative.

4. *Resolution*. This should be your ultimate goal, but it takes time to identify your anger and then resolve it with the person who is the object of your anger. Sometimes it may seem that you will never be able to go to your spouse, admit your anger, and work through the problem. Resolution may not occur until you are ultimately reconciled or divorced. You are not responsible for the other

person's response, but you are responsible to resolve your own feelings of anger. *The Anger Workbook* by Les Carter and Frank Minirth offers healthy ways to express and control your anger. It may help you identify and modify the anger that now prevents you from moving to the next stage in the grieving process.

Stage 3: Bargaining

During the third stage of grieving, called bargaining, anger mellows, and we begin looking for a simple solution to a complex problem. Some people see drugs, alcohol, or temporary superficial relationships as a solution for their problems. Some may even drown themselves in work rather than face the problems ahead. Others will bargain with the mate, trying to find a solution to make this all work out. Many try to do some bargaining with God.

During this stage, people say things like the following:

- "If you just come back, I promise never to drink [do drugs] again."
- "I'll do whatever you want if you'll just go to counseling with me."
- "You can have the house, the car, anything you want. Just let me have the kids."
- "If you move back in, we can go on like nothing ever happened. I promise, I'll never ask you about *her* again."
- "Lord, if You just bring him back, I'll go to church every Sunday. I'll even teach Sunday school."

There is a danger that during this time, some may try to reconcile too early. A separated couple may make a hurried attempt to patch up their differences without examining the issues that drove them apart. Things will not work out just because they move back into the same house and try to bargain their way into a workable marriage. Reconciliation takes two people committed to breaking out of old patterns and dedicated to giving time and energy to the task of making something better and more meaningful than they had before. It's much more than trying to resuscitate a dying relationship. It's the resurrection of a vital, growing relationship founded on forgiveness and changes in attitudes and behaviors.

By bargaining, you are trying to regain control of a situation that is out of control. Though a necessary step toward wholeness, it is during this time that foolish mistakes can be made. Out of desperation, you may become involved with a simple solution that has long-lasting negative effects. It is possible to compromise your self-esteem, your morality, your future financial security, and even your faith.

Lisa had the perfect simple solution: "Maybe if we just sold our single-level house and bought a two-story, things would work out. My husband could live upstairs, and I could live downstairs. That way the kids could see him whenever they wanted, and he would be there to watch the kids when I go to work. I wouldn't have to do *everything*. He could help the kids with homework." Lisa even went so far as to have her house appraised and spent a day looking for two-story houses that might fill the bill. She soon discovered she could never afford to make a move to a larger house. That made her stop and think: *How would I feel when his girlfriend came over to visit him upstairs? What if he wasn't always there when I needed him to be with the kids? Who would fix the meals? Would he expect me to do his laundry? What if he didn't want to help the kids with their homework? Would I get angry all over again?*

What seemed such a perfect solution one day suddenly

had major drawbacks. Be careful that you don't do anything out of desperation that you'll regret later. You are
not without resources. God Himself offers to give you wisdom: "If any of you lacks wisdom, let him ask of God, who
gives to all liberally and without reproach" (James 1:5).
Think through the options available to you and solicit
advice. Share your solutions with a trusted friend, and seriously consider the opinions offered. This may even be the
time to consider professional counseling.

When is it time to see a counselor? The Bible says, "He
who heeds counsel is wise" (Prov. 12:15). Tim Jackson in
his booklet on counseling says not to wait until you are in
a full-blown crisis situation. Seek help early: "When you
feel that something is bothering you, but you aren't sure
what it is; when you feel that everyone is against you;
when you keep hearing from others that you're being
unreasonable or insensitive; when you are unable to
change behavior that is harming yourself or others; when
you have thoughts of not wanting to live."[16]

Here are some situations that might call for the perspective and help of a professional. If you are not progressing
through the stages of grief or if the intensity of your grief is
unbearable, don't be ashamed to ask for help. If friends are
advising you to see a counselor, maybe they see a need in
you that you can't see. If there is no one you trust enough
to share your feelings with, a professional counselor might
be able to provide a safe place for honest sharing. If the
techniques you used in the past to cope with stress are not
working, perhaps you need someone with training to help
break down your seemingly impossible situation into more
manageable chunks.

If you don't know a professional counselor, ask your pastor, physician, or friends for a referral. Have a list of questions ready to ask, such as, What is your training, and how

do you view the counseling process? What is your availability? Cost? Payment expectations? Are you a Christian? Regardless of what others say, you need to be comfortable and trust the person you are going to work with. If after two or three sessions you are uneasy, don't hesitate to repeat the process until you find someone who meets your needs. Good Christian counsel can direct you to the power of God to face your trials—directed to look beyond your assets to see the resources of God.

Stage 4: Depression

During the stage of depression, you will be dealing with your situation realistically for the first time. You will no longer deny the reality of your broken marriage, try to blame someone else for it, or make bargains to solve your problems. Although the truth about your marriage may be discouraging, it is nonetheless *the truth.*

Depression is more than a day full of sadness or just feelin' blue. During separation, depression comes when you believe you are helpless—helpless to change your spouse, in-laws, children, and so on. Perhaps you are being forced against your will to move, get a new job, or change your standard of living. You may want to give up on everything. You may believe, *What's the use anyway? I'll never be worth loving again. I can't imagine ever being happy. Everything is overwhelming, and I don't trust anyone or anything. Why should I try to make new friends? I'm sure they'll let me down, too.* This sense of helplessness often brings on guilt.

At this stage there is danger again that some may consider methods of escape that are harmful, perhaps turning to drugs or alcohol or considering suicide. Others might escape by isolating themselves from any personal interaction, perhaps by sleeping all day long. If you have a family history of depression, have considered suicide, or have been severely depressed without any noticeable progression toward resolution, get professional help as soon as possible. Sometimes there are biological reasons for prolonged depression. I heard that an estimated 35 million people suffer from winter depression. These people become severely depressed (even to the point of considering suicide) due to a decrease in light. You may need only a visit to your family doctor to help you eat better, cope with allergies, sleep properly, or discover you could try light therapy.[17] Don't be afraid to ask for help.

About eight months after my husband left, I became depressed. I realized nothing short of a miracle would restore my marriage. One thing that kept me going was the discovery that I wasn't alone. I attended a workshop for separated persons in a neighboring church where I met people dealing with the same issues I was. If you haven't considered it before, perhaps this would be a good time for you to look for a workshop or even an ongoing support group to attend.[18]

Depression isn't pleasant, but it is a necessary stage in the grieving process. Your circumstances fill you with despair. You feel your pain deeply and are afraid it will never go away. When you reach that point, it's time to look up! In this psalm, David encourages us,

> O LORD my God, I cried out to You,
> And You healed me. . . .
> Weeping may endure for a night,
> But joy comes in the morning (Ps. 30:2, 5).

Start looking up and benefit from God's promises.

Stage 5: Acceptance

To this point, we have discussed the four stages you must go through to fight against what has happened to you. Each stage is a struggle. What happens if you have not dealt fully with the issues in a particular stage or have suppressed your feelings (even unknowingly)? Eventually, you will find it necessary to work through that stage thoroughly before you can finally begin to work on the final stage of the grieving process called acceptance. You cannot complete the fifth stage of grieving until you can answer the haunting question, Will I be divorced or reconciled?

Sometimes even after that question has been answered, a person can avoid true acceptance and, instead, choose resignation. My long-time friend Connie has been divorced for twenty years, yet she has never achieved acceptance. When she received her divorce papers, she said, "Life is over for me." She became a financial burden to her adult children and day after day sits isolated, filled with self-pity in her one-room apartment. Pat also chose the path of resignation, although she and her husband reconciled after a six-month separation. Two years later she told me, "I'm just so glad I'm not single; I prefer to continue with things as they are instead of facing up to the hard work it would take to make things right."

Legal complications or personal convictions may extend the time it will take you to work through the acceptance stage. After one year of separation, Julie wanted to get on with her life, yet she was stuck because of her spiritual convictions. She told me, "Until I see my husband actually marry the woman he left with, I don't feel free to move on." Out of a sense of obedience to God, Julie believed she must wait. She didn't want to make herself available to someone else until she knew her husband was no longer available to her. She entered the acceptance stage but couldn't move on. She wasn't denying reality and had, in fact, worked through every other stage of the grieving process, and had accepted the fact that reconciliation was very unlikely. Two years later when her husband did finally remarry, she was able to resolve her grief completely.

When you realize you have done all you can before the Lord and your spouse, you have no need to continually revisit issues of the past. You can move on with your life. When you discover you are no longer working through the issue that hurt your marriage, but instead are walking in a new direction with a smile on your face, you have truly reached the end of the grieving process. Even when you have completed the process it doesn't mean that you will never again experience sorrow or pain over the past or that you will never again feel anger toward your spouse but that you won't be consumed by those feelings. You will be strong enough to deal constructively with the painful memories and momentary frustrations and to move on with confidence, whether you are reconciled or divorced.

In the end maybe you'll have a visit with God as I did: "Lord, You know I never planned to be a single parent, but that's what I am. I won't fight it anymore. I can actually see some advantages to it. I still have questions, but one thing is for sure: I have more faith in Your plans than in any of my own. If Your plan for me is to stay single, that's just fine. In fact, I'm rather liking it."

That prayer didn't come quickly or easily. I don't believe I was ever stuck in any particular stage, yet it took me close to three years to complete the stage of acceptance and honestly say those things to both God and myself. I had to realize that what the future held wasn't my business: It was God's. I needed to be able to say along with the apostle Paul, "I have learned in whatever state I am, to be content" (Phil. 4:11).

One of the best gifts you can give yourself is permission to grieve. *Your pain identifies you—your choices will direct you*. Denial, anger, bargaining, or depression may identify you right now. Allow yourself to feel the pain, and go *through* the process of grieving to discover healing. You'll realize that you aren't alone. Even our Lord Jesus was "a Man of sorrows and acquainted with grief" (Isa. 53:3). What a relief to know you can go to Him, recognizing that He understands exactly how you feel.

God knows not only how you feel, but He loves you with a love that you can *never, never* lose. We've spent a lot of time focusing on what you've lost. Take a moment and consider what you can never lose: "I am persuaded that neither death nor life, nor angels nor principalities nor powers, nor things present nor things to come, nor height nor depth, nor any other created thing, shall be able to separate us from the love of God which is in Christ Jesus our Lord" (Rom. 8:38–39).

> *Dear Lord, I'm relieved to know that You designed this grieving process and that my feelings are normal. Help me to live one day at a time and to put my assurance in Your plans for me. May my loss be turned into gain as I more fully understand the depth of Your great love for me. In Jesus' name, Amen.*

AS YOU'RE CHOOSING TO GRIEVE, TAKE TIME TO CONSIDER . . .

1. How do you feel now that you know that it takes at least one or two years to go through the grieving process? Encouraged? Discouraged?
2. How long have you been separated? Are you ambivalent about how you want to see your separation end?

3. Who decided to leave the relationship? Why?

4. Do you think the grief of losing a relationship is harder to bear than the grief associated with the loss of life? Why?

5. When did you begin your grieving process?

6. What manifestations of grief have you experienced? Do you identify with one particular stage of grief at this time? Which one?

7. What fears are keeping you from moving through the stages of grief?

8. Can you identify the person(s) you are angry with? How are you expressing your anger?

9. What have you used to bargain with? Did it work?

10. What are some of your simple solutions?

11. Have you been depressed? If you have, how long? Do you see good coming from it?

12. What do you think your life will be like when you reach the stage of acceptance?

SURVIVAL TIPS

During your grieving process, you will spend most of your time wondering what happened. Here are some survival tips that I have collected over the years that have helped many separated folks get through this tough time.

• Start a list of the people who say, "Call me anytime if you need to talk," or "Let me know if there's anything I can do." When you think there's no one in the world who cares, get out your list, take them at their word, and pick up the phone.

• Change your environment. Rearrange your furniture. Hang a new picture. A new look may be just the lift you need to come home to.

- Get some exercise. Take a bike ride; go for a walk or a swim. Ever tried your hand at tennis, bowling, or skating?

- Eat healthy, well-balanced meals, and take vitamins. Watch your caffeine intake.

- Get adequate rest. If you're tired and time permits, take a nap.

- Write things down—everything from appointment times to when the videos are due. There is a sense of well-being when you can cross something off a list.

- If you know your day holds something unpleasant, do it as early as possible. If you get it over with, you will be freer to enjoy the rest of your day.

- Take advantage of your lunch break at work. Get away from your work area in body and mind. Moms who don't work outside the home need to do the same.

- Write down your feelings. You can throw the paper away or start a journal to chart your personal growth. Writing out your thoughts helps to clarify them.

- When you feel tense, try an old relaxation technique: Inhale deeply through your nose to the count of eight. Exhale slowly to at least the count of sixteen through tightly pursed lips. Repeat several times until you feel relaxed.

- As time and finances permit, get out of town. New sights and sounds can give you a new perspective.

- Try to do something that you enjoy every day. It can be something as simple as baking your favorite cookies.

- Do something to improve your appearance. Try a new look, hairstyle, or fashion. When you know you look better, you feel better.

- Read a good book, a humorous book, a joke book, or a good story that will help you laugh and forget about your pain for a while.

- Do something to promote growth in your life. Expand your mind by learning something new about cooking, world affairs, investments, stargazing, and so on.

- Delegate responsibility—sometimes you'd be surprised how much your children are capable of doing if you'd just give them the chance.

- Watch something grow. Plant a garden or just a seed in a pot by your windowsill.

- Do something for someone else. Take soup to a sick neighbor; watch someone else's children; invite someone to your house for dinner.

- Look for times to celebrate. I took the children out to their favorite restaurant (good thing it was cheap) on *our* payday. We celebrated making it through another two weeks together. We also celebrated good report cards, winning ball games, the first day of spring, and the last day of school. A bag of chips and sodas can go a long way.

- Accomplish something you had planned to do prior to your separation. Organize the closet, paint a room, or make needed repairs.

- Establish a routine schedule so things can run smoothly when you're not emotionally fit. Lay out your children's clothes in the evening (yours, too, if it helps). Set the breakfast table at night and even make lunches. On a day you have fewer commitments, cook and freeze extra food.

- Make plans ahead of time for the days you know will be difficult: the day your children return from visiting their other parent, birthdays, holidays, and so on.

- Create an environment of peace. Unplug the phone. Light a fire. Play encouraging praise music. Light a candle.

- Relieve your mind regarding locking yourself out of the house or car by making a duplicate set of keys. Carefully hide the extra house key outdoors, or better still, give it to a trusted neighbor. Carry an extra car key in your wallet separate from your other keys.

- Place God's promises in front of you throughout your day. Print out cards with verses that are meaningful to you. Pull them out during the odd moments: at a stop light, while you're waiting in line, or when you're washing dishes.

- Get up fifteen minutes early and give yourself private, quiet time to gather strength for the day. Spend time in prayer and perhaps read from the Psalms.

- Write out a list of blessings. Refer to the list when you're down, and add to it regularly.

NOTES

1. Tim Jackson, *How Can I Live with My Loss?* (Grand Rapids, Mich.: Radio Bible Class, 1992), p. 12.

2. Ibid., p. 6.

3. Bob Burns, *Recovery from Divorce* (Nashville: Thomas Nelson, 1992), pp. 175–77.

4. William J. Worden, *Grief Counseling and Grief Therapy* (New York: Springer, 1991), p. 22.

5. Ibid., pp. 23–24.

6. Ibid., p. 25.

7. Ibid.

8. Ibid.

9. Ibid., pp. 25–26.

10. Ibid., p. 26.

11. Ibid., pp. 27–29.

12. Sheldon Vanauken, *A Severe Mercy: Davy's Edition* (New York: Harper & Row, 1980), p. 184.

13. Gary Richmond, *The Divorce Decision* (Dallas: Word, 1988), p. 63.

14. Bob Burns and Tom Whiteman, *The Fresh Start Divorce Recovery Workbook* (Nashville: Oliver-Nelson, 1992), p. 28.

15. Charles Swindoll, *Three Steps Forward, Two Steps Back* (Nashville: Thomas Nelson, 1980), p. 150.

16. Tim Jackson, *When Help Is Needed* (Grand Rapids, Mich.: Radio Bible Class, 1993), pp. 24–25.

17. "Today Show," February 7, 1993.

18. Fresh Start Seminars, Inc. offers weekend seminars for divorced and separated persons in churches throughout the eastern and southern parts of the country. For more information about Fresh Start, write Fresh Start Seminars, Inc., 63 Chestnut Road, Paoli, Pennsylvania 19301, or call 1-800-882-2799.

CHAPTER FOUR

Choose to Look at Your Value

"Look, Mommy, look!" I heard a small child shout as he pointed to his sand castle. "It's the best I've ever done!"

"You sure are a good builder," commented a passerby as she strolled on the beach with children in tow. "Maybe you can use this." She handed him a feather.

"It's perfect now," he said as he placed the feather on top. "Come see, Mommy!"

The child ran up from the shoreline to where his mother was sitting on the dry sand. He grabbed her hand and turned around in time to see the wave roll over his beautiful creation. His mouth dropped open in disbelief as he stared at his flattened castle with only the top of the feather peeking out from under a mound of wet sand.

"What happened, Mommy? No waves came when I was making it."

"It's the tide, honey," she began to explain. "It's rising."

"What's a tide?" Not waiting for an answer, he ran back

to the place where his castle once stood. As he hurled sand bombs, he yelled, "I never really liked it anyway!"

The bombing ceased. Five minutes later he began to reconstruct his castle. As he firmly patted down the base, his older brother bent down next to him. Shaking his head back and forth, he said, "You shouldn't make your castle in the same place."

"Why not?"

"Another wave can come up and wreck it. You need to build in a different place . . . higher up . . . unless you want to watch it wash away again."

As I watched these children on the beach, I realized I had once been like that small child. My self-image was like his sand castle. I had built up my self-concept and was very proud of it. The encouragement and applause I needed to keep going were supplied by my spouse, family, friends and even an occasional stranger. After years of working on my creation, I was basically satisfied. Suddenly, without warning a big wave hit. The tidal wave of separation knocked my entire castle flat, leaving nothing behind. Then just like that little boy, I began to throw sand at my creation. I'd look in the mirror and say, "I never really liked you anyway. No wonder no one else does, either. You were never worth working on from the start." I had built my castle on the wrong foundation. I had been oblivious to the rising tide. I didn't even know there was a tide. I, too, would need a few tips from others before I began to rebuild my castle.

You are facing choices, too. You can remain ignorant about tides. If you choose to ignore the fact that tides do exist and decide to rebuild in the same place, be prepared to watch it wash away again. Eventually, another wave will come and destroy your castle. The next tide may bring the unexpected wave of financial ruin, physical disability, unemployment, illness, a wayward child, or the death of a loved one. The waves will roll in.

I like the big brother's advice: "Build in a different place . . . higher up." You can choose to rebuild your castle safe from destruction on a new foundation. Jesus told a story of two builders. He said the foolish man built his house on the sand, and the wise man built his house on the rock (Matt. 7:24–27). As you begin rebuilding your self-concept, you have the chance to work in partnership with the Draftsman of your castle. What an opportunity! He knows the design even better than you do!

WHY DO I FEEL BAD ABOUT MYSELF?

Prior to my separation, I had not known the meaning of the word *failure*. Oh, don't get me wrong. I had failed, just like everyone else. There were the times I didn't make the grades, didn't get the raise, didn't qualify for the loan, didn't get the job, but I had never interpreted my failures as a reflection of my personal worth. You see, despite my failings, the foundation I had chosen was still supporting me: The significant others in my life were still validating me. Therefore, my positive self-image remained intact. Separation was the first failure in my life that had left me questioning my value: If I'm really worth something, why did my "best fan" get up and leave? Not only had I failed at something, but I believed I, too, was a failure.

Maybe, like me, you have spent your life building your self-image on the feedback you received from others. Initially, it was my parents, then my peers, and then my husband. I evaluated how I was coming along based on my ability to meet the standards I had set for myself. Society influenced those standards through TV, school, family, and friends. Society tried to sell me the lie that my value could be found in my appearance, ability, affluence, and aptitude. Those untruths were supported everywhere I turned by both bold and subtle messages. I measured up to the superficial lies for nearly thirty years until the wave hit!

The wave of separation rarely washes away only a corner of the castle. My castle had been completely ruined with only a feather left behind. I might have been able to hide some failures from others in the past, but there was no hiding the fact that my husband had left me. Divorce and separation are public displays of very private matters. My separation made me open to public scrutiny. Others could make judgments about me and my personal life based on the condition of my marriage. When someone's name is on the front page of the local paper for a noble effort, that's one thing, but to feel as though the headlines read, "JAN'S A FAILURE—HER HUSBAND LEFT," is quite another. Because of my new (yet undefined) social standing, I felt exposed at work, in my neighborhood, even with my family and church friends.

Some of the feelings of vulnerability were imagined, but others were confirmed by the statements and questions of others: "Did you leave him, or did he leave you?"; "What could have been so bad that he wanted to leave?"; "I have always wondered why you married him in the first place"; "Have you had problems for a long time?"; "I noticed you stopped coming to church together. Is that when the problems started?"

I felt rejected both by society and by significant others who had once validated me. I was devastated when my friends let me down. Rejection came at unexpected times. I was ignored by some as if the condition of my marriage were contagious. I became a threat to other women. Becky called me to respond to a party invitation and said, "Now that you're kind of available, I don't know what's going on in my husband's mind. I'm not sure we'll be able to make the party." Becky was unsure of the stability of her marriage, and she directed her fears toward me. I might be the very one to steal her husband away, leaving her to experience a heartbreak similar to mine.

WHY DO I FEEL GUILTY?

The origins of guilt are complex. Guilt may be the result of something you've done wrong or the result of something you've done right! *"If only* I'd suggested we see a counselor," Gail said to me, "maybe he wouldn't have left. I feel so guilty for being the one who asked him to go. Certainly, that's not how a Christian wife is supposed to act. I've felt guilty now for six months. Is there any way out of this?"

Maybe you did something wrong, such as commit adultery, and you rightfully feel guilty. Or perhaps you've actually done something right. Often we allow ourselves to feel guilty for the wrong reasons. You may have been an enabler for years and finally took the necessary action to face the problems in your marriage, but you feel guilty. You also may have guilt that has no relation to your marriage. There may be issues relating to your work or other relationships, or you may have guilt over spiritual matters.

All kinds of people, not just religious people, feel guilty. Moral people feel they have let down their families and children. They might have thoughts such as: *I should suffer for what I did. I'll probably feel guilty for the rest of my life, but that's OK because it's what I deserve.* Guilt is the result of knowing you have fallen short of God's expectations or your self-imposed ideals, but that's OK because it does have a purpose. It moves you to look at your shortcomings. It reminds you of your need for forgiveness and points out your need for change. You can't go back and undo the past, but you can do something about the future.

Many separated adults find it difficult to move forward to build on higher ground because they are unwilling to take the time necessary to examine their values and understand their essential nature. Rather than wait to discover their value to God, some will look for something else to make them feel better quickly. They use many psychological defenses to hide their guilt rather than admit it. This is the time some people use alcohol or drugs to escape. Others may withdraw by burying themselves in their work or a new interest. Still others may rationalize their guilt and feel they are justified in quickly seeking a new relationship. Rather than face their shortcomings, some will project their guilt onto others: "If it wasn't for what my spouse did, I wouldn't feel this way." There will be those who will even try to make atonement for their shortcomings by holding on to their guilt until they've suffered enough.

WHO AM I?

Maybe, like me, you feel you are a failure. You feel alone and exposed. Possibly, your guilt has revealed your shortcomings, and you want to feel better. Don't wallow in your sense of failure or hide behind your guilt. Discover who you are. At a conference several years ago I heard of a helpful illustration that involved three circles, one inside another. Let's imagine a golf ball. Have you ever taken one of those things apart? Picture the small center core and label it "Who I Am." Next, see all those bits and pieces that look like rubber bands all glued together? Label the middle layer "What I Can Do." Now comes the outer shell; label this part "What I Have." The two outer circles represent the way you present yourself to the world.

"What I Have," my accumulated treasures and possessions, is readily seen by all. Some possessions I was born with: looks, brains, talents, and capabilities. Some treasures I've accumulated or constructed myself: my job, my house, my car, my children, my marriage.

When the superficial outer shell is peeled away, others will soon discover "What I Can Do." Some of "What I Can Do" will be dictated by "What I Have," such as my God-given talents, physical and intellectual capabilities. The remainder of "What I Can Do" is the result of how I choose to use my abilities. You can see how well I can do in parenting, maintaining a home, serving my church, making money, saving money, influencing others, and keeping my marriage together.

When a golf club hits a golf ball too hard, the ball is split open. If the protective shell is peeled off, the next layer is completely exposed. The rubber bands start popping off, and soon you're left with the center core. Separation can act like that golf club. It can split you open and begin the process of peeling away your layers of protection.

Once the center core of "Who I Am" is exposed, you have options. Your natural tendency might be to try to tape up the damaged ball or add some glue to the rubber bands to prevent the inner core from being exposed. You can do a patch job, quickly filling your layers of "What I Have" and "What I Can Do" based on your previous set of values. It may work for a time, but it is not a long-term solution. A patch job leaves you damaged and unable to fly straight and true when the next golf club strikes. Your other choice is to rebuild your life around a new set of values.

WHO REALLY LOVES ME?

God's view of you is vastly different from that of society and your significant others: "For the LORD does not see as man sees; for man looks at the outward appearance, but the LORD looks at the heart" (1 Sam. 16:7). If you choose to believe that God's estimation of you is far more important than what society and others think of you, a good self-image is possible. You will discover that you are His design, worth dying for, a new creation, in process, and that you have a special purpose. Understanding His acceptance of you will help you accept yourself and stop concentrating on the if only's of the past.

You weren't just thrown together. You were skillfully made. Look at Psalm 139:13–16:

> For You formed my inward parts;
> You covered me in my mother's womb.
> I will praise You, for I am fearfully and wonderfully made;
> Marvelous are Your works,
> And that my soul knows very well.
> My frame was not hidden from You,
> When I was made in secret,
> And skillfully wrought in the lowest parts of the earth.
> Your eyes saw my substance, being yet unformed.
> And in Your book they all were written,
> The days fashioned for me,
> When as yet there were none of them.

Your height, build, complexion, and hair color and quantity (or lack of it) are unique to you. In fact, God said He created you "in His own image" (Gen. 1:27). You were designed by the infinite Creator of the universe, and you bear His image!

The Bible says that God created no two of us alike, that

He fashioned our hearts individually (Ps. 33:15). Jesus said, "The very hairs of your head are all numbered. Do not fear therefore; you are of more value than many sparrows" (Luke 12:7). Get the point? You are of infinite worth to God. You are loved not because of what you have or don't have (e.g., your marriage), or what you can do or can't do (e.g., fix up the relationship), but because of who you are. You are His child (1 John 3:2). You are the object of His affection. You are a valuable, precious, unrepeatable creation of God.

The love of God is *unconditional*. God's love is everlasting (Jer. 31:3). In Romans 8:39, we are told that absolutely nothing shall be able to separate us from the love of God. That's good news. We will never be denied God's love. Only sin can keep us from a relationship with Him.

God desires a relationship with His valuable creation. However, there can be no relationship with Him unless we admit that we haven't lived up to His standards. This disobedience is what God calls sin. The nature of God is holy (Lev. 19:2). The nature of people is sinful (Rom. 3:23). That is what separates people from God. God, however, is eager to be reconciled with you. His plan for your reconciliation is a gift. You're worth so much to God that He sent His Son Jesus to die for your sins (Rom. 5:8). Punishment for everything you should feel guilty about—past, present, and future—was taken care of by Jesus. He took all your guilt and sin into His sinless body and was judged as God required: He died. But the good news is that He rose from the dead three days later! God was satisfied, and now the way is clear for your relationship with God to be restored.

I've heard it said that the unbelievable truth of Christianity is this: God loves you so much that Jesus Christ would have died on the cross even if you had been the only one! When you refuse to value yourself as God does, in essence you are telling Him that He made a mistake in sending His Son to die for you. There is no sin too great or too small for God to forgive. The moment you choose to enter into a relationship with Him by recognizing your sin and accepting His plan of reconciliation you are instantly a new creature. At that point you also enter the lifelong process of becoming more like Him. Not only do you have the wonderful privilege of being in a relationship with God here on earth, but you have the promise of spending eternity with Him (John 3:16).

I met Peter at a seminar. He asked me, "If I can't measure up to the standards of society, how can I ever measure up to God's standards?" The answer is simple: You can't. You'll never be perfect this side of heaven, but you can be forgiven. You no longer need to strive for acceptance. You are accepted because of who you are. You can be forgiven for everything you have done that is sinful. Just ask and you'll see!

HOW CAN I BECOME A CHILD OF GOD?

Everyone has different reasons initially for choosing to come to God through Christ. Some desire nothing more than to have an assurance of their eternal destiny. Others want comfort in the midst of grief. Some see Christ as hope in the midst of despair. There are those who want relief from guilt through His gift of forgiveness. Some desire to know truth. Many want to change their lives and walk in a new direction. I'm sure the list goes on.

I entered into a relationship with God as a nine-year-old child after responding to a message I heard at summer camp. The process of becoming like Christ, however, didn't begin in earnest until years later when I was knocked flat by the tidal wave of separation. It was then I realized along with the psalmist: "It is better to trust in the LORD than to put confidence in man [or woman]" (Ps. 118:8).

I attended church regularly through my high school days and early into my marriage. A few years prior to my separation, getting to church became difficult. It was hard to leave my first baby in the church nursery. Since both my husband and I worked, I was reluctant to spend half of our only day off together in church. Neighbors were upgrading their homes, and we wanted to keep up. As I filled my "What I Have" circle with a newly remodeled home, spa, sod lawn, and a new car, I needed to earn more money, so I began to work on Sundays. The excuses made it easy to stop going to church.

Even though I was pursuing false, human values with great gusto, I knew exactly where to run when the tidal wave hit. I remember one morning I woke to a silent house. It seemed so strange to have the children spend the night at their daddy's house. I felt alone and full of despair. I reasoned that I might never make sense of my separation, but there was something I knew for sure. My prayer went something like this: "Jesus, I know I've turned my back on You lately, and I'm sorry. I believe You are who You said, the Son of God. You promised You would never leave me, and I believe You. I don't want to go through this all by myself. I need You! I'm willing to live my life the way You want me to from now on. Thanks for putting up with me. Amen."

I believed God was stronger than I was and He would see me through whatever lay ahead. I chose to turn to God because I knew He loved me and could be trusted. I had a history with Him. At this point you may be asking yourself, How could I ever have enough faith to believe like that? That's OK. Give yourself permission to doubt. In the next chapter we'll talk about faith: what it is and how you can develop it.

You become a child of God when you choose to believe in Jesus and accept His love for you (John 1:12). God says you are a *new* creation (2 Cor. 5:17). When you believe in Christ as Savior, you are spiritually transformed. You're not merely renovated or repaired; you receive a brand-new nature, a fresh existence (Col. 3:9–10; Rom. 6:6). Christ offers you a new past and a new future (Rom. 6:1–6; 8:18–32). You have a new relationship with Him (1 John 1:1–4). You have a new source of provision and inheritance (Phil. 4:19; Eph. 1:11). God created you for His own pleasure (Ps. 149:4). He seeks your worship and praises, and He desires that you glorify Him by fulfilling His purpose for you (John 4:23; Ps. 50:23). You are a residence for God Himself (2 Cor. 6:16; 1 John 4:15); He makes your heart His home. You are worth so much to God that He chooses to live inside you. His other creations don't have that opportunity. That's more than a compliment; it's a complement!

You have a new family (1 John 3:1). This new family will help affirm your decision to accept God's value of you and encourage you as you begin the process of becoming more like Christ. God created you with a specific part to play in His church, which is pictured in the Bible as His body. In 1 Corinthians, we learn that this body has many parts and that every part holds equal value. It goes on to say that the body won't function properly unless all the parts are working together doing what they were created to do (12:14–17). You were created to be a functioning member in the body of Christ. Read these verses, and then try to dispute that you are important and that you have a purpose.

IS THE STRUGGLE OVER?

To be in process is both comforting and unsettling. It is comforting to know that because God cares about me, He is in the process of making me more like Himself. It is comforting to realize that God looks at my potential, not just the way I am today. But I know that the work He's doing won't be accomplished easily—and that's the unsettling thought: "Do not be conformed to this world, but be transformed by the renewing of your mind, that you may prove what is that good and acceptable and perfect will of God" (Rom. 12:2). Don't be discouraged when you don't see immediate changes. It takes time to accept your new identity and learn how to renew your mind. The transformation doesn't happen automatically. It happens as you continually renew your mind with the Word of God, not the word of people. You are given one chance after another to believe or not to believe what God says about you. You can believe what He says about your position in Christ, or you can choose to believe what your feelings, friends, enemies, or circumstances might say. Choose consciously to think about who you are in Christ, and wait on His ability to help you be everything He desires (2 Cor. 3:5; Phil. 4:10–13).

We read in Philippians, "He who has begun a good work in you will complete it" (1:6). He *will* complete the job, but He's still working at it. We're all unfinished! He's working to conform us (Rom. 8:29). The process might not be easy and you might not feel comfortable, but that's OK. God didn't come to make us happy, but rather to change us. When I feel worthless, I am forgetting that God Himself is working on me. I am concentrating on the part that isn't finished yet rather than on the part that is being shaped. I am allowing someone or something to make me feel inferior. As Chuck Swindoll said, "No one can make you feel inferior without your consent."[1]

Why should I resist these feelings of self-doubt and accept God's plan to work on me? Because He truly knows the best way to forge my character, to build it up and temper me. There are many times I need to persevere in the process. The apostle Paul said, "Tribulation produces perseverance; and perseverance, character; and character, hope" (Rom. 5:3–4). We find the key that unlocks the door to hope through persevering. Choose to persevere with Him through this refinishing process. Choose to become a partner with a God who loves you too much to leave you the way you are.

Dottie, a fifty-four-year-old woman, told me she had invited God to help her change while she was waiting for her husband of thirty years: "It isn't easy, but I guess I'm just persevering at this point. I went back to school, lost fifty unneeded pounds, and joined a Bible study. I'm not sure if my husband will ever come back. Nevertheless, I have a new sense of who I am. I have confidence in God's power, not my own."

Looking to fulfill your heavenly purpose doesn't mean you won't be any earthly good. It means you have a purpose in life beyond a merely selfish existence: "God wants us to feel good about ourselves. But, He wants it to be on His terms, not ours."[2] When you give God credit for who you are, you can be secure about yourself. When you love and value yourself, you are free to love and value others. When you think well of yourself, you bring glory to God, in whose image you are made.

Your pain identifies you—your choices will direct you. Your failure and guilt can help identify you as a sinner. What you choose to do with your sin will direct you. God wants you to have a new set of values that will withstand the next wave. Don't settle for society's cheap, quick fix.

Dear Lord, help me to see myself the way You do. Help me to change my perspectives. Help me to wake up each day and clearly see Your purpose and love for me. Let me never forget that Your gifts are free for the asking. Help me to accept them eagerly. In Jesus' name, Amen.

Perhaps you have never made the decision to enter into a relationship with Jesus. The following prayer will guide you to that place of reconciliation:

Dear God, I admit that I've done wrong. I know I need a Savior, and I believe that Jesus Christ died for me. Come into my life and forgive me. I receive You now as my Savior and the director of my life. Thank You for new purpose, for hope, and for assurance of my salvation. In Jesus' name, Amen.

WHILE YOU'RE LOOKING AT YOUR VALUE, TAKE TIME TO CONSIDER . . .

1. What values do you use to measure your self-image?
2. If you could draw a graph of your self-image over the years, how would it look?
3. Have you ever been hurt by the reactions of a significant other in your life? By society?
4. How can you develop an accurate self-image?

5. What are your treasures in the layer of your life labeled "What I Have"?

6. What are some of your abilities in the layer of "What I Can Do"?

7. Do you think a sense of failure can help you gain a new positive self-esteem? How?

8. What do you feel guilty about? Is your guilt a result of something you did wrong? Something you did right? Do you feel forgiveness is possible?

9. Do you feel worthy of God's love? His forgiveness? His offer of a new life?

10. Have you ever accepted God's gift of reconciliation through Jesus Christ?

11. What is God in the process of completing in you?

12. What is the purpose in your life?

NOTES

1. Charles Swindoll, *Three Steps Forward, Two Steps Back* (Nashville: Thomas Nelson, 1989), p. 135.

2. Martin R. De Haan II, *How Can I Feel Good About Myself?* (Grand Rapids, Mich.: Radio Bible Class, 1988), p. 12.

CHAPTER FIVE

Choose to Stop Worrying

"Hello, I'm responding to your baby-sitting ad." A quiet, female voice continued, "Are you still looking for someone?"

"Oh, yes," I replied. "I need someone as soon as possible."

We agreed to meet the next day at a park close to her apartment so the children could play and we could talk.

She was waiting on a bench and greeted the children with a warm, "Hello, my name is Crystal." Curly dark hair and long beaded earrings framed her plain eighteen-year-old face. Her only makeup was light pink lipstick.

"Want to go for a swing?" she asked my three-year-old daughter.

"Oh, yes. I love to swing! Would you push me?"

"Of course! I love to push kids who want to swing."

We walked over to the playground equipment. Crystal quickly removed her sandals and settled my daughter in the swing.

"Higher, higher," my child yelled with glee.

"Do you have experience with little children?" I asked.

"No, not really, but I'm willing to learn. It could work out good for both of us since I need to move out of my apartment this week and you need someone right away."

The idea of trading room and board for baby-sitting seemed the perfect solution to one of my daily worries. My shift work as a nurse was from 6:00 P.M. to 6:00 A.M. It seemed an impossible task to find a sitter who would spend the night and then stay on through the next morning to watch the children as I slept. Friends had told me, "Don't worry, Jan. Just have faith; things will turn out all right." I knew I was God's child, with new purpose and hope, but I wondered why I was still so full of worry.

Back home that evening, the phone rang. "Hello, this is Crystal. I'm ready to move over to your place. I'll be there anytime between eight and two o'clock tomorrow."

At three o'clock the next day, Crystal stood on my porch surrounded by an assortment of packing boxes and books. "Where shall I put my juicer?" she asked as she walked in.

I led the way to the kitchen. "There's room here on the counter," I said as I quickly moved cookbooks and a plant. I had never thought through the implications of sharing my house with someone else's *stuff*.

"Where shall I put my vitamins?"

I pointed to the counter. "I guess they can go along with the juicer for now."

Crystal came back with an armload of textbooks. "Are you aware of the great value in seaweed?" she asked.

"No, not really."

"This will tell you all about it." She flung a pamphlet on the dining table in front of me.

"Do your kids get very many colds?" she asked as she

walked over to her box full of vitamins. "If they take a large dose of this zinc every day," she said as she held up a bottle, "they'll *never* get another cold!"

"It's not that easy. I'm still breast-feeding my son."

"Then how in the world will he ever get all his vitamins?"

That evening as I was driving to work I reminded myself of my belief in God: *He loves me and promised to take care of me. I did all I could to prepare Crystal; she seemed attentive and eager as I went over the instructions.* Then I prayed, "OK, God, I've spent most of my life worrying; I think it's really a pretty bad habit. I'm ready to quit. I want to trust You and Your ability to care for me, but I'm not quite sure how. So here goes. . . . You're in charge."

I was not prepared for what greeted me when I returned home. It looked as if every toy we owned along with various pots, pans, and spoons had been dumped onto the floor. I stepped over parts of games and puzzles, assorted books, records, and crayons as I made my way to the other end of the kitchen. I glanced at the sink piled high with dirty dishes. In the overflowing trash basket, I noticed an empty wine bottle hiding under some discarded pieces of children's artwork. *Oh, Lord, is this the way You care for my children when I choose to trust You?*

After a deep breath, I walked slowly into the living room. I didn't know if the alcohol would make her violent, so I measured my words carefully. "Crystal, what happened here?"

She sat in an overstuffed chair with an unopened magazine in her lap. She shifted, looked up at me with dull eyes, and answered, "I let them play with whatever they wanted. They seemed to be real happy."

I dropped my purse and ran to the children's bedroom. They were both soaking wet, but sleeping peacefully. *Safe!*

Now I could pray, "Thank You, Lord, for keeping them safe. I need Your help to know what to do now."

I walked with determination back to the living room. "Why did you put the baby to sleep without any plastic pants?"

"Oh, I guess I just forgot them." She was still sitting in the chair, staring out the window.

"It looks like this baby-sitting work is harder than you thought," I said.

"Yes, there's just so much to remember."

We were both very quiet. After a moment, I said, "I think we both gave it a try, and I'm sorry it won't work out. You can stay for two weeks if you need to while you look for another place to live." I didn't want to treat her unfairly, but I knew I could not leave my children in her care again.

"But what will you do about a baby-sitter?"

In the past I often had asked myself the same question. With confidence I had never before experienced I said, "Crystal, I truly believe God knows I need a sitter. He'll help me. One thing I'm not going to do is to worry. I guess I'll have to go back to my daily telephone routine to look for sitters."

"I thought you told me before that I was an answer to prayer . . . and you don't like me. I'm a failure. How can you say God helped you?"

I felt it was an honest question from a troubled heart. I wanted to give her an honest answer: "Crystal, it's easy to think that God has vanished and hasn't lived up to His responsibilities when things don't turn out as I plan. I'm learning, though, to see that when we commit ourselves to Him, He does have a purpose for everything. Sometimes we see the purpose right away; other times not for a long time. I thought the purpose of our meeting was to give you a place to live and to give me a sitter. Instead, the purpose for our meeting may be for you to hear about Jesus and for me to learn how to stop worrying by having faith in God."

The discussions Crystal and I had over the next two weeks led me to look more closely at my habit of worry. I remembered the Bible verses that said, "Do not worry about your life" (Matt. 6:25), and "Be anxious for nothing" (Phil. 4:6). I wondered what God might do to me if I continued to worry. Things *were not* turning out all right; in fact, things were a mess! I prayed, "Lord, do I just need more faith so You will take me out of this mess?"

WHAT IS WORRY?

Dave Egner in his booklet *What Can I Do with My Worry?* says, "Worry is how we express our fear of the future. We're afraid of the consequences of what lies ahead."[1] In the Bible, the Greek word for worry means "to be anxious, to be distracted, to have a divided mind."[2] Where there is worry, the attention is divided—one part of the mind is busy worrying. That Greek word is used to describe two kinds of worry. One kind is actually beneficial and positive. It can be expressed by our English word *concern*. In 2 Corinthians, Paul said that on a daily basis he had a "deep concern" for all the churches (11:28). The churches' welfare was always on his mind, distracting him from other thoughts and duties. Out of his concern came many beneficial and positive actions and prayers for the sake of others. However, in Philippians, Paul used the same Greek word when he said, "Be anxious for nothing" (4:6). In other words, don't worry. *Worry* is a good word to describe this harmful, negative, and even disabling kind of distraction. Nothing good comes from this type of anxiety until it is transformed by God.

WHAT DO I WORRY ABOUT?

Sometimes we worry about the consequences of a bad decision. We may realize, in the instant or in retrospect, that we have not taken responsible and appropriate action in response to a concern. We worry when we realize we may have failed. These fears are often related to the if only's in our lives: "If only I had studied harder for the test"; "If only I had put more money in the parking meter"; "If only I had checked Crystal's references more carefully"; "If only I had insisted we go to a counselor when I knew our marriage was in trouble."

We also worry more or less vaguely about situations that *could* bring us physical, emotional, or spiritual harm. An illness, a change in the economy, or a realignment of personnel at work could leave us unemployed. A fire, tornado, earthquake, or flood could leave us homeless. A drunk driver could leave us, or our loved ones, injured or dead. Harsh, degrading comments could leave us humiliated. Marital separation could leave us divorced—and alone.

Unexpectedly, my vague fear of separation became a reality. I had many concerns and many questions. You may also have many of the same concerns, concerns that relate to you, your spouse, your children, and God. "I've been so deceived. I don't know how I can ever trust a man again," said Marcie. "I've never worked," a middle-aged woman confessed to the group. "I'm worried that I'll grow old and be penniless." "I feel so sorry for my husband. He's done this to himself," Elsie said, "but I'm worried about him. He has nowhere to go, no one who really cares about him." "I will always feel responsible for what my children are going through," Suzanne said. "They never asked for this, never deserved it, and had nothing to say about it. How will it affect them when they get older?"

Sometimes a relationship with God seems to add to our worries. "How can separation or divorce ever glorify God?" Melinda asked. "I told my family that I became a Christian. Now, here I am, the only one in the family with a failing marriage. I've really let God down!"

WHAT DOES WORRY ACCOMPLISH?

Jesus said we worry because we doubt and don't have faith (Matt. 14:31). Doubt comes when we are double-minded, divided, and unstable—distracted (James 1:6–8). We cannot focus our attentions on God because we don't trust Him to run the world effectively, let alone our lives. Instead we trust our plans, our work, our money, our spouses, our families, and so on. Indeed, God gives each of us opportunities to exercise authority and take on responsibilities, but much of life is beyond our strength and skills—beyond our control.

Sometimes we naively think if we just had enough money, we would not be vulnerable because all our problems would be solved: We could buy health for our children; we wouldn't need jobs; we could repair any tornado damage; and we know rich people have perfect marriages. The truth is, money is not enough. Some things are irreplaceable, and some things are not for sale. When our marriages get into trouble, we realize how little control we have. We cannot make our spouses love us and be partners in relationships they want no part of.

Jesus said not to worry because it won't change a thing (Matt. 6:25–34). We can never control what will happen to us by worrying. Our concerns, however, can motivate us to take action for the safety or well-being of ourselves or others, thus lessening the impact of our regrets about whatever does happen and what we should have done about it. Warning signs should alert us to danger. Out of concern, not worry, we need to take responsible and appropriate action: Dismiss the baby-sitter when we recognize her incompetence, have the brakes checked when they squeak, fill up the gas tank when the gauge is near empty, see the doctor when we are sick, and seek out professional help when our marriage is in trouble.

WHAT DOES TRUST ACCOMPLISH?

"All I want is a job," Beverly said. "God knows I need one. I've given the whole situation to Him. In fact, I keep giving it to Him . . . and nothing happens. It's making me lose my faith . . . *whatever* that is. If He's supposed to be in control, why are things even worse?"

When we make the initial decision to trust in Christ, there is an implication that our future will be changed. We monitor that change internally by our attitudes and emotions. Three words are involved in learning to stop worrying: *belief* (or its verb form, *to believe*), *faith*, and *trust*. We often see these words used interchangeably because they have similar, interconnected elements. *Webster's Dictionary* says *trust* is "a firm *belief* or confidence in the honesty, integrity, reliability, justice, etc., of another person or thing; *faith*; reliance."

The writer in Hebrews says, "Without faith it is impossible to please Him, for he who comes to God must believe that He is, and that He is a rewarder of those who diligently seek Him" (11:6). Faith is obviously a necessary element in the life of a Christian, but at first glance it seems ethereal and vague. The word *faith* was used only twice in the Old Testament. It was expressed and encouraged, however, by such words as *trust* and *believe*.[3] Faith begins with believing. Early Christians were simply called "believers."[4]

Belief is defined as the conviction or an opinion that certain things are true, but faith is more than an intellectual assent. The demons don't have faith, but the Bible says they believe—and tremble (James 2:19).

A step beyond belief is trust, which implies commitment because of the reliability of someone or something. The Hebrew verb for trust means "to place one's hope in, to go for refuge, to have confidence in." Trust is the interpersonal element of faith; it is the way I relate to God. If I am trusting, I "have faith."

Biblical faith involves a commitment to what we believe, based on persuasion, not force.[5] I have seen this commitment compared to embarking on an airplane trip from New York City to Paris.[6] After you buy a ticket and go to the airport, it is pointless to sit at the terminal saying, "I believe the airplane can fly; I trust the pilot; I'll get to Paris if I just get on the airplane." You must act on the facts you believe to be true: You will prove your belief by getting on the plane. You might get on the plane confidently and be worry free, or you might get on the airplane reluctantly and worry. Either way, you are on your way to Paris (Lord willing; see James 4:15)!

How can we ever overcome our doubts or worries? The director of a program that helps phobic and panicked fliers says that aviation education is the key to helping these people overcome their fears. The more a fearful flier knows about how a plane stays up in the air and what turbulence is, the more the person can relax and stop worrying.[7] So, too, it is with placing your faith in God:

> Trust in the LORD with all your heart,
> And lean not on your own understanding;
> In all your ways acknowledge Him,
> And He shall direct your paths (Prov. 3:5–6).

This passage tells you to trust in the Lord. If you want a relationship with God, first you must have knowledge about Him. Then you must act on that knowledge by making a commitment, just like getting on the airplane. The result will be this: God, not you, will direct your paths. You will gain the confidence to trust and stop worrying by putting into practice what you continue to learn about your relationship with God. You will be free from the distraction of the past and the future and will no longer have a divided mind. We become single-minded as we choose to trust God (Matt. 6:22).

WHOM CAN I TRUST?

From my open window I could see that the recent rains had filled the drainage ditch at the back of our neighbor's property with three feet of rapidly flowing water. It was a welcome and rare sight in our drought-stricken state.

"I'm going to make a bridge to get to the other side of the ditch," I heard ten-year-old Andrew announce to his mom.

"Oh, I'm coming, too. I'll help! I'll help!" his younger brother Michael yelled. I saw them dart off to their woodpile, slamming the door behind them.

"Think this one will work?" Michael asked. I watched as they carefully inspected the old two-by-four boards. Together the boys selected and carried off a heavy board, cautiously placing it over the ditch of swiftly moving water.

Andrew yelled, "OK, Michael, you can be first."

Michael took one step out on the board. He looked down at the cold water five inches below him, then back to his house. He stepped back and said, "I don't think I trust it. You go first!"

"No problem," Andrew said with confidence. "I trust it. I've done this lots of times!"

It would have been foolish for Andrew to prance out onto the board, expecting it to hold him up if he hadn't inspected it first. The greatest amount of faith in a damaged board would have been no help. Andrew could have started to walk boldly across on a weak, split board but soon would have discovered it wouldn't support him. In contrast, even the smallest amount of faith in a solid piece of wood would have held him up in fine fashion. Often the question is not, Do I have *enough* faith? Rather, it is, Is the object of my faith trustworthy?

Michael was too young and immature to know what he was looking for. He thought he had faith in the board after carrying out an inspection, but then he was unable to follow through. He feared to cross the ditch on it. Andrew, on the other hand, was older, and he knew to look for cracks and knots that might mean a weakened board. Michael wanted to trust the board, but he doubted. He was fearful, and he worried. He looked to his brother to prove to him that the board was trustworthy and would hold him up.

Like Michael, we, too, may spend time inspecting spiritual truths without really knowing what to look for. We, too, need examples to follow. In the Old Testament, God spoke to His people through the prophets (Heb. 1:1). Few saw God as openly as Moses: "The LORD spoke to Moses face to face, as a man speaks to his friend" (Exod. 33:11). But in the New Testament, God, in the person of Jesus, revealed Himself face-to-face to thousands of people (John 14:9). Jesus is described as being "the brightness of [God's] glory and the express image of His person" (Heb. 1:3). Jesus explained how to come to God and how to follow God's ways. He is not ashamed to call us brothers and sisters (Heb. 2:11). We are fortunate to have such an "older brother" to trust and follow, even though we haven't seen Him with our physical eyes (John 20:29). As we get to know Jesus better through Bible study, prayer, and fellowship with others, we will gain the confidence to trust Him, and we will want to follow through with action: That is what we call faith.

HOW WILL MY FAITH GROW?

"Mommy, after we finish reading this book, I'd like a snack, OK?" My four-year-old daughter crawled under my covers and snuggled up next to me.

"Sure, honey, what would you like?" I asked.

"How about some cookies in a bowl? That way I won't get crumbs in the bed."

"Sweetheart, I'm so sorry. Mommy ate them all up last night."

"Well, how about some crackers? Only, I mean the good ones that I like." After a moment of silence, she said, "No, I guess I don't like crackers. I know. How about some Jell-O?"

"We don't have any," I said. "Your brother finished it all for lunch."

"How about some applesauce?"

"I'm sorry. We don't have that, either."

"Mommy, I have a good idea. Why don't *you* tell *me* what *I* want?"

I chuckled and then thought maybe my daughter could teach me some lessons about how to trust. She had made the choice to trust me with her request, believing that I had the wisdom to match her desires with what I had in my cupboards. She placed faith in me to provide sufficiently for her. Could I admit that I really don't know what God has in all His cupboards? Could He have something that I would want—something I would never know to ask for? I concluded that I needed to learn how to trust God like my daughter trusted me.

Jesus said unless you humble yourself and become as a little child, you will not enter the kingdom of heaven (Matt. 18:3–4). As I watched how my children placed their confidence in me over and over again, I discovered many *favorable* childlike qualities like trust that I could incorporate into my adult life.

Children start as little babies and grow into adulthood. If we are to become as children, we, too, should expect growth in our lives. We need to put away childish things and grow up (1 Cor. 13:11). Growth implies different levels of skill and learning. That was the difference between Michael and Andrew as they inspected the board. Faith is a dynamic and growing adventure. None of us are instantly mature adults. Likewise with faith, none of us are instantly mature Christians. Next time, Michael might go ahead and walk out on the board but still have doubts. That's not a sign that he has failed or is faithless; it's merely a reflection of his immaturity. As he grows up, he'll know more about inspecting boards. Faith grows from taking action on what we know at the time.

WHAT CAN I EXPECT, WHEN I TRUST GOD?

Separation forces adjustments on everyone involved. The problems each one faces are different, based on unique circumstances. The Bible never says that if we trust in Jesus, our problems will be over. In fact, in some cases, problems increase, and things get rougher. Having problems means we are human, not necessarily unspiritual. In the book of James, we learn that God actually uses trials to test our faith to produce patience and complete the process of transforming us (James 1:2–4).

As God teaches us through our problems and concerns to recognize our inadequacies, we can choose to trust Him to provide for our needs and to liberate us from our fears and worries. Crystal wasn't God's solution to my problem, but my needs were always met. He answered my prayers by making sure I had plenty of names of sitters to call; occasionally, I was able to trade shifts, making it easier to find help; assistance came in unexpected moments from neighbors and friends. God wanted me to grow up: He wanted to change *me*, not the circumstance.

My children trust me to love them, provide for them, guide and direct them. I know, despite my best efforts, at times I have failed and will continue to fail them. God will never fail them. Neither will He fail you or me. Do not fear to place your confidence in His sovereign ability to be in control of your life. He knows what's best because He knows what's in the cupboard! To trust in God is a *daily* decision to place your confidence in His plans and resources. It's not a one-time decision that frees you from worry; it's a choice that must be made every time you face the pressures and trials of living. In the midst of trouble you can have peace of mind and freedom from the distraction of worry.

The peace found in Christ is a peace the world doesn't understand (John 14:27). It's not a peace that comes from ignoring the situation or from exerting your will and determining to be peaceful. It is a peace that comes from trusting God (Isa. 26:3). He has both the interest and the ability to care for you and to help you when circumstances are out of your control.

Knowing God has the ability to control the days you

can't and then choosing to trust Him to do so are the first steps toward peace and freedom (Job 22:21; John 8:32).

HOW WILL I FEEL WHEN I CHOOSE TO TRUST GOD?

I watched my children in the driveway. The jump rope slapped on the cement with an even rhythm. "It's your turn, Mary. Jump in." The song began, "Mary and Johnny, sittin' in a tree, K-I-S-S-I-N-G. First comes love, then comes marriage, then comes Krissy in the baby carriage!" All the girls giggled.

That's how it is—sometimes. Our culture believes that "first comes love, then comes marriage." In the movie *Fiddler on the Roof*, we see another way. Papa believes there is just as much validity in "first comes marriage, then comes love." Both sequences result in recognized marriages. A commitment to Christ has similarities to both of these marriage arrangements. For some, there are passionate feelings that spark a decision to trust Christ. For others, the choice is based entirely on facts.

Our culture places a high value on feelings. Be careful not to judge the validity of your spiritual decision based on your feelings. "I think I *should* feel something," Judy admitted, "but I don't." Maybe you, too, have accepted God's love, confessed your sin, believed in Jesus, asked His forgiveness, and accepted His gift of salvation, but like Judy, you really don't feel any different. Don't worry! Joy can come immediately or later, but it will come. It's hard to make progress in life based on feelings alone. You can't place your faith in your feelings; they change from moment to moment. Your faith must be in something that never changes: the trustworthiness of God and His promises, as revealed through Jesus Christ. In the next chapter, we'll look more closely at the promises of God and discover facts about who God is.

Your pain identifies you—your choices will direct you. During separation, concerns come along that easily can become distracting and disabling worries. The worry itself becomes another source of pain that points us to God for relief. Worry can be replaced by faith. The adventure of faith begins small as a simple belief, but it grows to maturity as we choose to follow Jesus. God does have a plan for you, and when you choose to trust Him, He *promises* to direct you. He knows what's in the cupboard.

> *Dear Lord, help me to stop trying to control things You never intended me to control. I have lots of concerns, lots of fears, and lots of worries. I want to trust in You. Give me the strength I need to wait on You and to step out in faith to trust in Your ability to direct my days. In Jesus' name, Amen.*

WHILE YOU'RE CHOOSING TO STOP WORRYING, TAKE TIME TO CONSIDER . . .

1. What are your concerns right now?
2. What can you do to keep your concerns from becoming worries?
3. What do you worry about? What are you afraid of concerning your future? Your spouse's future? Your children's future?
4. Where or to whom do you go when tragedy or pain comes your way?

5. How well do you know God? What will it take to get to know Him better?

6. Can you name a time you offered your all to God? Was it based on facts or feelings? How do you feel now?

7. Do you believe God knows what's best for you? What do you think He might have in the cupboard for you?

8. What areas of your life are hard to trust God with? Do you have to feel good about God to trust Him?

9. How would your life be different if you chose to trust God to run your life?

10. Is there reason to be concerned about your Christian witness?

11. What can you thank God for?

12. Do you think God is trustworthy?

NOTES

1. Dave Egner, *What Can I Do with My Worry?* (Grand Rapids, Mich.: Radio Bible Class, 1992), p. 13.

2. W. E. Vine, *An Expository Dictionary of New Testament Words* (London: Oliphants, 1965), pp. THO-132, CAR-168.

3. J. D. Douglas, ed., *The New Bible Dictionary* (Grand Rapids, Mich.: Eerdmans, 1971), p. 410.

4. Ibid., p. 412.

5. Vine, *An Expository Dictionary of New Testament Words*, pp. OBE-124, PER-179.

6. Kurt De Haan, *Can Anyone Really Know for Sure?* (Grand Rapids, Mich.: Radio Bible Class, 1987), p. 11.

7. Kathleen Doheny, "Fear of Flying: 1 in 6 Are in White-Knuckle Club," *Los Angeles Times*, October 25, 1992, section L5.

CHAPTER SIX

Choose to Get Serious with God

"Good-bye, Daddy, have fun at the party!" Our three-year-old daughter wrapped her arms around my husband and squeezed tightly.

"Thank you, honey, I'll try. When I come home, I'll come in and give you a kiss. I promise."

"Oh, good," she stepped back and looked up at him. "I always sleep gooder if you kiss me when I'm sleeping."

"You're going to Joe's new place, right?" I asked.

"Yep, he's supposed to be all moved in."

It seemed odd that my husband was going out with the guys on a Friday night. It was something he had never done—had never seemed to want to do—in the eight years of our marriage. Yet now things were different; he was restless.

An hour later the phone rang. "Hello, this is Richard.

I'm a client of your husband. I'd like to meet him at his office first thing in the morning. It's very important."

"I'll have him get back to you as soon as he can."

I thought I should try to reach my husband so I picked up the phone again.

"Hello, Joe. This is Jan. I hear you're moved in and celebrating. I need to speak with my husband, please."

"Well, I am all moved in." There was silence. "I canceled the party today at work when I realized not very many could make it. I'm sorry to tell you," he hesitated again, "your husband isn't here."

My mind was suddenly awhirl. I tried to sound unconcerned as I said, "I guess he could still be on his way. If he comes, just tell him I have an important message from a client."

It was difficult to concentrate on reading my book the rest of the evening. *Did he just forget the party was canceled, or did he deliberately lie to me?*

I heard the dead bolt turn in the front door. The clock read 11:30. My heart began to race, and I suddenly found it hard to swallow. I heard him walk slowly down the hall and into our daughter's room. *He didn't forget his promise to kiss her good night. Maybe all my questions are needless. He probably hasn't broken any promises to me, either.* He walked toward our room and stopped at the doorway.

"I didn't expect that you'd still be awake."

"I just got going on this book and couldn't put it down. How was the party?"

Walking past the bed and into the bathroom, he said, "Oh . . . it was OK."

I spoke loud enough to be heard over the running water, "Did you ever get the message that I called you?"

He turned off the water and walked quickly to the bedside. "You actually called Joe's house?" he asked in disbelief.

"Yes," I answered.

He started to walk away. I called out, "Wait a minute . . . don't go." He turned around. Looking straight into his eyes, I said, "I *know* there was no party at Joe's tonight. So where did you go?"

"I knew the party was canceled," he said, "but I needed to go somewhere . . . anywhere alone. I didn't really know where I was going when I left here, so I just decided it was best to let you think I was at the party. I ended up going to a movie." He drew a deep breath and, looking at the floor, added, "It wasn't even any good."

"I don't care that you went out. I didn't even care that you were going to spend time with the guys. I don't care that you ended up at the movies. I *do* care that you told me one thing and deliberately did another. I can live with almost anything but not a lie."

"But I didn't lie to you on purpose," he said. "I just didn't know what else to do."

My eyes filled with tears, and my voice was weak as I asked, "Do you expect me to trust you again? You're making me think I'd be pretty stupid if I did."

WHY ARE PROMISES BROKEN?

I thought that I knew my husband, that he was committed to me and would never leave me. I was wrong; he left. I thought that I knew God, that He would never leave me. Would I be wrong again? Could He leave me if He wanted to? I wanted to trust my husband, but I discovered facts that indicated he could not be trusted. I also wanted to trust God, but I was afraid I might learn that He could not be trusted, either. Since I doubted His ability to help me today, how could I ever trust Him with my future?

My husband and I had dated four years prior to our eight years of marriage. I knew we had broken many well-intentioned promises to each other, but always there had been reasonable explanations. But now, something in our relationship had changed.

My husband's words and character had previously inspired confidence; I trusted him completely. When I discovered that he had lied to me, I found myself questioning everything he said. Because my understanding of commitment and loyalty had been shattered, I became unsure of my ability to distinguish the truth.

I felt compelled to examine my trustworthiness. I had thought that my words and character inspired confidence and that I could be trusted completely. I could always be trusted to show up for work, to pay my bills on time, to remain faithful to my spouse. After an honest appraisal, however, I realized that certain circumstances could change my attitude about my promises and commitments.

People make all kinds of promises. Promises declare the perceived values of the giver and the receiver of the promise. Promises reflect the skills, abilities, and intentions of the promiser. Not all promises are kept, though. Sometimes promises are broken *because we're weak*. Even though we try, and we have every good intention, we fail: "I promised to go on a diet, but I just can't stop eating my favorite candies"; "I promised to stop drinking, but I just can't seem to do it"; "I promised to love you forever, but I've fallen in love with someone else." By the actions we take and the choices we make, our weaknesses are displayed for others to see.

Sometimes we break promises *because we're enlightened*.

We recognize a bad promise in light of new information or developments. I've made many bad promises over the years, and I've tried to learn from them. Even though they were innocently made, my poor judgment hurt others. I am reminded of one such promise I made a few years ago to my son. Tears poured down his face.

"But, Mommy, I don't understand. You *promised* we could have my party in the park!"

"Honey, I didn't know it was going to rain. I can't stop the rain. Even if it does stop in time, I can't dry off all the grass, sand, and play equipment. We can't have the party in the park today."

No matter how hard I tried, I couldn't make him understand why we couldn't have the party in a wet park. My unqualified promise should have had some qualifiers; I realized I had made a bad promise.

In a marriage, one spouse's weaknesses and subsequent choices may persuade the other to break a good promise: "Since you choose to continue to drink, I now choose to quit enabling you . . . I'm leaving"; "Since you love someone else, I now choose to stop loving you as my spouse . . . in sickness and in health . . . till death do us part." Unexpected events and new facts cause us to change our minds regarding the wisdom of keeping a promise.

Promises may be made under duress only to appease someone else; we really never had any intention of keeping them: "I promise to see a counselor"; "I promise to look for a job"; "I promise to break it off with my boyfriend." In essence these promises are being broken as they are being spoken.

Similarly, we make empty promises to make someone else feel better, or perhaps we don't know what else to say: "I promise; things will be all right"; "It'll be a girl this time; I promise."

Making a promise should be taken seriously because a promise is an obligation for which we are held accountable. Since promises are meant to be kept, every time we break one, sin is involved: lack of character, poor judgment, carelessness, outright deceit, and more.

IS IT RISKY TO BELIEVE GOD'S PROMISES?

Does God face the same limitations that people do when He tries to keep His promises? My son trusted my promise about his birthday party, and I failed him. I trusted my husband's promise regarding his love, and he failed me. How much of a risk was I taking if I chose to believe God's promises?

It takes courage to trust when we are conscious of what's at stake: job, house, children, marriage, future. We feel at risk when our doubts are aroused or we begin to count the cost. Risk is measured by uncertainty plus the value of the goal or object. Sometimes risk is masked by overpowering emotions that confuse our thinking: "I'm willing to continue with my affair because I don't think anyone else needs to know, and I need to lie only a little." Sometimes we decide a risk is worth taking because of other benefits: "I'm willing to live in California, even though I could be in an earthquake." Sometimes we don't care about the risk because the value of the object is so small: "I'm willing to let you wear my jacket; it's no big deal if you lose it." And sometimes we are totally unaware that there is any risk, even though the loss would be significant: "We're lucky to be alive. The mechanic said our brakes are gone."

The more we know about the circumstances or the abilities of the one we trust, the smarter we can be about the risks we take. Since your separation, you have probably faced more changes than at any other time in your life. Great security and peace come when you know you can trust in God, who will never change His mind about keeping His word to you (Deut. 7:9; Matt. 24:35).

The Old Testament uses words such as *oath* and *covenant* to express God's formal agreements. However, even when God merely speaks, His words carry the weight of a promise because the words come from God's knowledge, power, honesty, and integrity. In the New Testament, we find a Greek word translated "promise" that specifically means this sort of announcement or message: God's promises *declare* His agreement to do or not to do something. Kurt De Haan in his booklet *How Does God Keep His Promises?* says, "The promises of God are the heart of the Bible. Everything God has spoken, every announcement, every message, is really a promise based on God's perfect, good, and trustworthy character."[1]

God gives us new values and removes uncertainty in our lives. He does so by giving us commands—guidelines to live by—and by giving us promises—mercies we will receive. His gift of mercy, in the form of His promises, gives us the courage to live life to the fullest. Let's look at God's ability to carry out these promises.

Since the creation of the world, God's attributes have been seen (Rom. 1:20). He invites us to know Him and benefit from all He has promised. He can never deny Himself; He can do nothing but remain faithful to Himself (2 Tim. 2:13). When we hear that God never changes (Mal. 3:6) or that "Jesus Christ is the same yesterday, today, and forever" (Heb. 13:8), do we understand what the statements mean? They do not mean that God is inactive or static (Heb. 4:12). They mean He will always be God and His characteristics will never change: He is always sovereign, always powerful, always loving, always holy, and always wise.

WHO IS GOD?

God Is Sovereign

The Lord is the God of all gods, the Lord of lords, the King of all kings, the Creator of all things (2 Chron. 2:5; Deut. 10:17; Rev. 19:16; Isa. 40:28). He reigns in heaven and on earth and will do so forever (Ps. 47:7–8; Luke 1:33). Because of His supremacy, we owe Him primary allegiance. God is jealous of His rights (Deut. 4:24) and asks that we give Him honor by worshiping only Him: not children, a spouse, money, a job, or a marriage. He makes plans for us because He has the right to. He is the King who supplies all our needs.

God has control over the good and the bad in our lives (Eccles. 7:13–14). It's easy to say God's in control when things are going well, but what do we say when we see trouble or are in trouble? Even though He could, God doesn't always fix things that go wrong in this world. (Sometimes it appears that He seldom does.) He gives us responsibility and choices that have consequences. He allows us to make mistakes and to create chaos by not following His instructions regarding how He intends us to live life.

Nevertheless, God, who is in control of all things, also gives us the promise that He will work everything together for good if we love Him and are called according to His purpose (Rom. 8:28). Even when things don't seem to be going well, they are still under God's control. Things still are fitting together in the big picture—we just don't see how! When you feel things are out of control and that nothing good can come from your separation, remember God is sovereign. He has the ability to work even your separation into His plans for good.

God Is Powerful

God makes plans for us because He is sovereign and, therefore, has the right to. His plans are carried out by His power (Dan. 5:21). When God spoke, everything was made out of nothing (Ps. 33:9), and everything continues to exist by His word of power (Heb. 1:3). God has power over the elements that He created. Jesus has that same power. Once He was in a boat with His disciples when a great wind suddenly arose. The boat was covered with waves. The disciples awoke Jesus and asked Him to help them. He said, "Why are you fearful, O you of little faith?" Then He rebuked the winds, and the sea and winds were calm (Matt. 8:23–27). Jesus also had power over unclean spirits. When He spoke, the demons departed (Mark 1:23–27). He had power over the devil himself when He was tempted in the wilderness (Matt. 4:1–11). He had power over disease and was seen healing many ailments (Matt. 4:24). There is nothing too difficult for God to handle (Jer. 32:17).

If we personally trust Christ as our Savior and Lord, we are told that Christ lives within us (Rom. 8:9–11). What does that mean? That same power that is in Jesus, the power that raised Him from the dead, *is in us* who believe (Eph. 1:19–20). There were days I hated to get up because I felt I had no strength to face the problems that would certainly come my way. Where would I get the strength to pray, to confront my husband, to be a patient mom, a productive employee, a good friend? God promised He would help me get through anything by His power (Phil. 4:13).

That promise brought me hope in those times of weakness:

> He gives power to the weak,
> And to those who have no might He increases strength
>   (Isa. 40:29).

God Is Loving

God's love for us is unconditional. There is nothing we can do to make God love us any more than He does at this moment. As we do with our own children, however, He may approve of our behavior more at one time than another; but His love is constant. God's love is eternal; He loved us before we even had our being (Jer. 31:3). He continues to express His love by offering mercy and forgiveness (Dan. 9:9).

When we look at Jesus, we can see what God's love is like. We learn about some of the complexities of loving in the story of Lazarus. Jesus received a message that His dear friend Lazarus was close to death. Because He was sovereign, Jesus was in control of the situation. He announced His plan to bring glory to God through the sickness, but Lazarus was dead by the time Jesus reached his home. There Jesus wept. Jesus loved Lazarus deeply and suffered along with everyone else who grieved over the death of Lazarus. Yet Jesus never despaired, for He had a purpose for all that took place. By His power, Jesus then raised Lazarus from the dead. It was in His timing, for His purpose, and with His love that He carried out His plan (John 11).

When I discovered God expressed His love this way through Jesus, I believed that He could have that same kind of concern and purpose for me, too. I was heartbroken and filled with fears, but God promised to be "near to those who have a broken heart" (Ps. 34:18). He promised that His love would cast out all my fears (1 John 4:18). I found my fears were gone when I remembered that God's plans are motivated by a love that always desires what's best for me.

God Is Holy and Just

"God is light and in Him is no darkness at all," declares 1 John 1:5. God is completely separated from evil and is righteous in all He does (Ps. 116:5). God doesn't struggle to maintain His holiness. He simply is holy, absolute purity. Because God is holy, He hates sin and must judge it. Though He loves the world, His justice dictates payment for sin, that is, death for the sinner. God's plan was made before the foundation of the world: The death of Jesus (who was sinless) on the cross made it possible for God to forgive sinners and still satisfy the requirements of justice. Jesus had to live a holy life to satisfy the law (2 Cor. 5:21). Thus, God could be faithful to His holiness and faithful to His love for His creation when He provided a means of salvation from His judgment against sin.

I needed to find this balance in my life. I spent needless time and energy trying to figure out how to "make my husband pay" for all I thought he had done to me rather than following the example of Jesus. Rather than condemn, just moments before His death Jesus asked the Father to forgive those who played a part in His crucifixion (Luke 23:34). Jesus had every reason to ask the Father to punish them rather than to forgive them. I realized the final judgment in my situation was God's, not mine. Were it not for Jesus, judgment would be coming *my* way.

God Is Wise

Knowledge is the amount of information we have. *Wisdom* is how we use that information. God alone has all wisdom: "The foolishness of God is wiser than men, and the weakness of God is stronger than men" (1 Cor. 1:25). He knows every step, every unconscious foot tapping, and everything you're thinking at this very moment (Ps. 139:1–3). He knows not only the minutest detail of your past, present, and future but also all the possibilities; He knows all your if only's (1 John 3:20). He sees the total picture of your circumstance.

You may have lied to your spouse, or your spouse may have lied to you. You may have lied to yourself, but you can't fool God with a lie because He knows you. You can be sure He will *never* lie to you because He is holy (Prov. 30:5). He sees the whole picture, and because He is wise, He knows exactly what needs to be done.

As I became confident in God's wisdom, I wanted Him to be in control in my life (no matter how bad things looked or how I felt). I wanted to benefit from His promise:

> Trust in the LORD with all your heart,
> And lean not on your own understanding;
> In all your ways acknowledge Him,
> And He shall direct your paths (Prov. 3:5–6).

HOW DOES GOD KEEP HIS PROMISES?

I still had some unanswered questions, even after studying God's attributes and discovering that He has the ability to keep all His promises. There were times it seemed God had let me down. Sometimes I felt His promises were empty because I thought what God had said He would do was not happening in my everyday experience. Maybe you feel God has broken some of His promises to you, and you question His ability to remain true to His word. Gradually,

I recognized that my problem was that I was trying to claim promises that He never intended for me! In time, I learned that God does exactly what He says He will do, to or for whom He chooses, in a manner consistent with His character, according to His timing. He is always faithful to Himself and to His creation.

God does exactly what He says He will do. He makes some promises to us that will be fulfilled, no matter what we do. These promises are unconditional: to send the Messiah, to send the Holy Spirit, to help us pray, to love us (Isa. 52— 53; John 16:5–15; Rom. 8:26, 39). On the other hand, He makes some promises to us that have conditions we must meet in order to receive the fulfillment: *If* we seek what has eternal value, God will take care of our temporal needs (Matt. 6:25–34). *If* we confess our sins, God will forgive us (1 John 1:9). *If* we ask God for wisdom, He will give it (James 1:5). *If* we love the Lord and are called according to His purpose, all things will work together for good (Rom. 8:28).

God speaks to a specific person or group of people. Not every promise in the Bible is intended for us personally. Just because you come across a promise that sounds as if it would be great, *don't assume it is intended for you.* Some promises were made to a specific individual or group: to Noah to rescue him and his family (Gen. 7:1), to Solomon to give him wisdom and riches (1 Kings 3:10–14), to Mary to give her a supernatural conception (Luke 1:26–38). You might be trying to make every penny count, and you get excited when you read God's promise to make you prosperous and give you a land flowing with milk and honey (Exod. 3:8). Read on, and you'll discover that promise was intended for the Israelites prior to entering the Promised Land. God made other promises that He intends for all believers: eternal life, the Holy Spirit within us, forgiveness, peace of mind, answers to our prayers, wisdom, and strength to do God's will (John 3:16; Eph. 1:13–14; 1 John 1:9; Phil. 4:7; Matt. 7:7–11; James 1:5; Phil. 4:13).

God will keep His promises in a manner consistent with His character. God always fulfills His promises, but He is not boringly predictable. The Bible is full of promises that have been fulfilled in obvious ways, but sometimes the ways are not so obvious. The greatest promises in the Bible concern the coming of the Messiah (Isa. 53; Matt. 1). The Jews were expecting a royal King to rule a political kingdom. God kept His promise to provide a successor to David's royal throne, but Jesus was unexpectedly born to a poor family and was called the son of a carpenter. Rather than rule as a king, Jesus lived as a servant and a teacher. Rather than conquer the Roman Empire, Jesus, the King of kings, died a disgraceful death. The Resurrection was the biggest surprise of all!

God keeps His promises according to His timing, not ours. For young children, time seems to go so slowly: "How many more days until we go to the circus? Is today the day? I can't wait!" For adults, time goes much faster, and older folks say it zooms by. Now imagine the age of God: No wonder our perceived idea of a short time is so different from His. No matter how long I think something *should* take, it's rarely the time frame God has in mind. And many times God fulfills His promises in ways we do not expect. God said, "For My thoughts are not your thoughts, nor are your ways My ways," to explain why we often do not understand how or why He acts as He does (Isa. 55:8). His plan of action is based not on how I think He should carry it out but instead on who He is. There is a time for everything, including God's timing (Eccles. 3:11). Our task is to wait—and to be obedient.

GETTING SERIOUS WITH GOD

I was elbow-deep in dishwater when the phone rang.

"Hello, Jan, this is Barbara. Bruce was just here doing some work for us. He tells me the two of you are talking about marriage."

I couldn't have been more shocked. *Where did he get that idea? What should I say? Could he actually be thinking of marriage?*

"I know you and Bruce have been spending time together, and I thought it was great to see you so happy. He's so good with the kids." She continued, "I have to admit, though, I was a bit concerned when he said you were talking about getting married. It all seems rather sudden."

"He may be thinking about marriage, Barbara, but it's the farthest thing from my mind. It's obvious he and I need to talk. Thanks for the call."

I went back to the sink full of soap suds. God alone knows how long I stared out the window thinking about my relationship with Bruce. I had been separated well over a year, and it was apparent that my husband intended to marry his girlfriend. He had yet to file for divorce, however, because he told me he "wasn't quite ready." I met Bruce, a divorced man, through a fellowship group at church. My children loved his attention. It always made their day when he stopped by to play with them. It made my day, too, knowing someone found me desirable and worth caring for.

Have I used my children as an excuse for spending time with Bruce? Have I done what makes me feel good rather than what I know is right? Am I free to date if I'm not free to remarry? We're not really dating, but we're spending time together. Have

I lost my hope that one day God will do a miracle and my hus-
band and I will be reconciled?

My eye caught sight of a lonely bird perched on the
branch outside my window. I whispered a prayer, "Lord, I
don't like being alone. It's nice having a little help to raise
these kids. I do care for Bruce. Maybe I even love him.
More than anything, though, I know I love the feeling of
being loved. It seems like I've been alone and rejected forever. I enjoy finding myself in Bruce's embrace followed by
a tender kiss. Is that so wrong?"

Where will our hugs and kisses lead? Is our physical relation-
ship too intense for our relationship to bear? Were we not
Christians, I know we would have taken things farther last
night. Maybe he sees marriage as the honorable step to take
before we compromise our values. I bet that's why he said what
he did to Barbara.

The rest of the day seemed as long as a week while I
waited for Bruce to drop by. There was so much I needed
to say. Where would I start? I don't know how many ways I
must have rehearsed my lines.

The doorbell rang. The kids ran to the door, announc-
ing, "It's Bruce, Mommy! It's Bruce!" He walked in, bou-
quet of flowers in hand, and offered me a warm smile as
the children jumped into his arms. His eyes seemed to say
much more, even as he said simply, "These are for you
because you're special. You're as beautiful to me as these
flowers."

How can I ever tell him that I'm not ready to promise my
life to him? I'm not sure why, but I know I'm just not ready. If
I'm honest with him, I could lose everything we have together. I
could be facing the future all alone. Is it worth it?

I watched the kids smother him with hugs and kisses. I
swallowed hard and felt sick to my stomach. I knew in my
heart that I couldn't make a deeper commitment to

Bruce—at least not now. I had to tell him. To let him think otherwise was unfair. To continue in our relationship without a willingness to commit more deeply to him was wrong. To continue the relationship to meet my needs was selfish and wrong. To continue the relationship because of the physical pleasure it brought was wrong. I felt certain, at the rate we were going, our relationship would lead to immorality. *What will I say?*

Bruce helped the children put a puzzle together while I fixed dinner and continued to think. *I need to get more serious with You, God, not with Bruce. Why is it always so hard to do what You want me to do?*

As I went through the nighttime routine with the children in their room, I could hear the crackle from the fire Bruce had started. After the children were settled, I sat next to him on the couch. "Bruce, there's something I really need to talk to you about."

"OK, shoot."

"Barbara called today. She said you mentioned to her we were talking about marriage. I've been thinking all day."

"Does that mean I'm going to hear your answer?" he asked with a grin.

"First of all, you've never asked," I said seriously. "Our relationship seemed to start out so pure. I've never shared my heart with anyone like I have with you. What we've shared has been wonderful. And I really do love you. But . . ."

He grabbed my hand and squeezed it tightly. A tear rolled down his cheek as I continued, "I can't commit myself to you. I'm still married to someone else. My marriage has to be over before I can even think of entering another one."

"The morning I met you I had been praying," Bruce

explained. "I told God I was ready to be married and have children. When I saw you walk into church that day, I thought you were God's answer to my prayer." His voice began to break. "I've never stopped believing that one day we'd be married."

"I'm sorry. I guess I've taken advantage of our relationship, and I didn't even know it. You have given me so much. I've learned about myself, about being honest and vulnerable, how it feels to be loved again. Our love has grown, but I can't say that I want to be your wife."

We stared at the hissing fire in silence for some time. *What was he thinking? Oh, no, what have I done?*

"Maybe because I had been waiting for so long, I sort of wished you to be God's blessing," Bruce admitted. "I can't believe you're telling me it's over. Maybe time will change things."

"Maybe it will," I said, licking a salty tear from my lips, "but don't make me go through this again, it hurts too much."

The truth is, I did go through that scene with Bruce time and time again. The same words, the same tears, and the same ache in my heart. I tried to break things off, but neither of us could totally let go of Bruce's wish. Eventually, however, the Lord through time convinced us both that we could never be married to each other. My sense of confusion and loss drove me once again to look closely at why it was so important to trust God's promises and obey His guidelines, even when that is painful.

WHO IS IN CHARGE?

Some commands and directions of God are not itemized. Nowhere in Scripture will you find specific directions and guidelines for dating while separated. Biblical scholars offer differing views regarding the freedom one has during a time of marital separation. Some say that if your marriage has been violated by adultery, you are divorced in the sight of God, no matter how long the state in which you live takes to make it legal: You are free in the eyes of God to enter another relationship. Others say that even if you are legally divorced, you are *never* free to remarry (or even date) unless your spouse remarries or dies: Until then there is always a chance for reconciliation.

I was not very aware of the arguments for and against dating while separated. Perhaps I should have been; I might have saved myself and Bruce some pain and struggle. Since that time, I have found a book with some straight talk on the subject. Written by Bob Burns and Tom Whiteman, *The Fresh Start Divorce Recovery Workbook* explains clearly that because "dating is a prelude to remarriage, not a therapy for reconciliation," if your marriage is not over emotionally, spiritually, and legally, you are not free to date.[2]

There are two undisputable commands you cannot ignore during separation. First, God has commanded that intercourse be reserved for marriage alone (Matt. 19:3–6; Mark 10:6–12). Second, He has commanded that we are not to allow ourselves to be driven by lustful desire, exploiting another person for selfish sexual pleasure (1 Thess. 4:5–6). I was personally made aware of God's commands for me through His Word and my own God-given conscience. I had a choice to heed the commands and warning and be obedient or to ignore them and be disobedient. For a greater understanding of this issue of sexuality, I encourage you to read *Sex & Love When You're Single Again* by Thomas Jones. It offers great insight into the whole arena of sexuality as a "single again" adult.

God's commands usually invite obedience through an

act of the will (trust, faith, choice), yet His takeover of our lives might seem like an overpowering invasion. He knows how to get our attention! During my separation, I felt forced to face God in a way I never had before. I related to the apostle Paul's famous trip to Damascus. When he left Jerusalem, he didn't have a clue about how drastically his life would change. He was stopped by a powerful vision of Jesus and temporarily blinded. That got his attention! But Paul was not *forced* to follow Jesus and become a believer. He was given a choice. He wisely recognized the truth and voluntarily became Jesus' servant, willing to obey a new set of commands.

Throughout Scripture, Abraham's belief and obedience are commended, particularly the faith in God he exhibited when told to sacrifice Isaac (see Gen. 22). Though God does not ask us to offer a child as a sacrifice on a literal altar, He does ask us to make sacrifices in order to be obedient.

The better I know God, the easier it is to make the choice to obey because, like His promises, His commands are based on His character. I continue to be amazed by the mysteries of His ways. He said that when we follow Him, the burdens we carry aren't nearly as heavy as before. What looks hard, even impossible, is actually easy to bear with Him. He actually says His burden is light (Matt. 11:30). I draw encouragement from that! I think He links promises and commands to further encourage joyful obedience: The burden of obligation is not all on me. If I meet my obligation and fulfill the condition, I will receive the benefit because God will meet His obligation and fulfill the promise. He is even willing to help me fulfill the condition because it is impossible to obey God in my own strength. He communicates and empowers me by means of the Holy Spirit (Rom. 8:5–9, 13–16).

WHY SHOULD I OBEY?

I have a purpose for almost everything I ask my children to do. Sometimes I must protect them from harm: "Don't touch the hot stove." Sometimes I want them to learn responsibility: "It's your turn to feed the dog tonight." When I issue a command, I expect obedience. When my children ask, "Why?" they don't always get an explanation. Sometimes they have to obey "just because I said so."

Likewise, God has a purpose in what He asks of us. When He gives commands, He asks us to trust Him. Obedience on our part is wise because only God knows the beginning and end of all things. He desires and expects our obedience based on His authority and the choice we made to become His children: "If you love Me, keep My commandments" (John 14:15). The Bible says we will know that we know Jesus if we obey Him (1 John 2:3–4). Our choice to obey Him pleases God. In fact, our obedience pleases Him more than any sacrificial offerings of the past (1 Sam. 15:22) because He wants a real relationship, not empty ritual. His purpose is for us to be mature.

I am reminded of a time my five-year-old son and I were out in front of our house. "Stop!" I yelled. He was fifty feet away from me on his bike. "A car is coming!"

My son was not obedient to my command, and rather than stop, he turned directly into the oncoming car. Luckily, the driver was going slowly enough to avoid an accident after she either saw him or heard me scream. I had a better view than my son did of what was going to happen, and I gave a command to protect my child. God also has a better view of things and wants to protect us (His children) from harm. He gives us commands to provide both immediate and eternal protection and peace. What security!

I saw what it would take to protect my son from a car accident, and I also knew what it would take to teach him road safety. He was told, "*Never* ride without Mom," and "*Never* go near the highway." Did that mean I would ride alongside him forever and he would never ride on a highway? Of course not. As he obeyed my commands, over time he would learn responsibility. One day he would discover the great benefits of riding his bike wherever he wanted.

Growth and maturity come through obedience as we apply what we have learned. There are times we allow our children to make a bad choice in order to teach them a lesson. There are even times we allow them to be slightly harmed: "Now you know what it feels like to get burned. When I say, 'Don't touch, it's hot—now you know why.'" I know what a joy it is to watch my children grow up. God must experience similar pleasure as we become more responsible and discerning, choosing to obey Him for the sake of love and wisdom rather than out of fear.

When asked why I obey God, I would like to think my answer is always, "I want to please Him and do what's right." Yes, there are those times, plenty of them. However, I realize that sometimes I obey God's commands because of the threat of punishment or a consequence I don't want to face: "I won't have sex with you because I don't want a baby or a sexually transmitted disease." The Bible says, "The fear of the LORD is the beginning of wisdom" (Prov. 9:10).

However, not all fear comes out of respect for God. Because of fear, many remarriages take place too quickly. There is fear that "no one else will come along and I'll be alone the rest of my life." At a conference I learned that after a divorce or separation, there is often a deep and meaningful relationship formed with someone of the oppo-site sex. This "special person" helps an individual to become (and to recognize) the "right person" suitable for remarriage. Some people mistakenly choose to marry this transition person. My friend Anne told me, "I knew in my heart that my present husband was a quick fix. He gave me the comfort I needed at the time. It seemed proper to marry him, but I moved too fast. We'll probably struggle in our marriage for the rest of our lives. I didn't trust God enough to wait."

God grows us up by His request for obedience, and He enables us to become like Him, to be holy (1 Pet. 1:13–16). We begin to reflect His character after the initial decision to follow Him; thereafter, we are further transformed each time we make the choice to get serious and obey Him. As we learn to be humble and obedient as Christ was (Phil. 2:5–8), we become partakers of more and more of God's holiness (Heb. 12:9–10).

Jesus set the example when He made "Himself of no reputation, taking the form of a bondservant. . . . And being found in appearance as a man, He humbled Himself and became obedient to the point of death, even the death of the cross" (Phil. 2:7–8). When we are humble before God, we will desire nothing else but to obey Him. Christian humility is the grace that makes us think no more highly of ourselves than we ought to think (Rom. 12:3), mindful all the while that we are sinful. We need this realistic awareness of ourselves, God, and others in order to empty ourselves of the privileges we thought we had and become a servant. Jesus instructs us, "Humble yourselves in the sight of the Lord"; He promises that when we do this, "He will lift [us] up" (James 4:10).

God's goal is not so much that we be happy and comfortable but that we change. When our goal is to glorify Christ and serve Him, we can expect to be transformed—

by whatever means God chooses. The pathway of obedience is not always an easy road marked with "happy face" smiling stickers; sometimes the road is marked by struggle and tears. When our perspective changes and we begin to see things from an eternal viewpoint, we can be obedient even in the midst of what seems a loss. We know God will use it for good in the future; He promised that!

WHY DON'T I OBEY?

If there are so many benefits to obeying God's commands, why don't I always obey? Why is it such a struggle to do what I know is good for me? When I am truthful, I discover that sometimes I have reasons, but sometimes I don't. Sometimes I don't know how to obey, and then there are times I think I just can't.

I Don't Want To

"But, Mom," yelled my six-year-old from his room, "I just don't want to get dressed. It's such a bore, just like a chore. Hey, listen, I made a rhyme! Mom," he waited for my answer, "I still don't want to!"

We could fill volumes of books with examples of willful disobedience on the part of our children. Could we fill just as many with adult examples? "I don't want to save myself until I get married." "I don't want to give the money my spouse deserves." "I don't want to stay sober and face my pain tonight."

I Didn't Hear You

My son's rhyme expressed an obvious lack of respect for me as his "commander." When we ignore God's commands, we are not showing proper respect to Him as our commander. Other than just not wanting to, why do I ignore God's commands? There are plenty of times when I say, "I just didn't hear You, Lord." I hear that excuse from my children all the time.

"Why don't you have your jacket?" I asked my daughter as she snuggled up close to me on the windy football bleachers.

"I didn't bring it, Mom."

"I must have said three times before we left, 'Go and get your jacket.' "

"Well, Mom, I guess I just didn't hear you."

I think it's selective listening rather than the fact that she never really heard me, but whatever the reason, the command was not heard. She was not listening and, therefore, did not take action. Do I ignore the voice of God?

I Don't Know Why

I slapped my five-year-old's hand for the second time and asked in frustration, "Why don't you obey Mommy? Do you like being punished?"

"Mommy, I don't know why I don't obey. I guess I just like to do what I like to do."

Doesn't that say it all? Sometimes we don't know why we do what we do, but we do it anyway (even when we know punishment is around the corner). Sin does that to us.

I Don't Know How

"Go ahead and print out your report," I said to my ten-year-old and promptly left the room to prepare dinner.

After about fifteen minutes, she appeared in the kitchen with a long face. "Mom, I don't know how to make the printer work."

Many times we are ignorant. Either we don't know what God's instructions are, or we aren't mature enough to

respond with confidence to His commands. We must communicate with Him through prayer and the study of His
Word. We need to watch others make it work, too, so we
will be prepared to obey the next time we're asked.

I Just Can't

The day was a blur. The car broke down; the dryer dried
the last load of its life; I burned the brownies. Then a call
came from school: "Your daughter is here in the office with
a temperature."

"OK. I'll be right there to pick her up."

"Go get in the car," I said to my son.

From the counter I picked up the videos to be returned,
grabbed a bowl in case my daughter was sick in the car on
the way home, and then headed for the coat closet. As I
reached in for my coat, my son appeared at my side,
returning from the garage. "I thought I told you to get in
the car."

"You did, Mommy, . . . and I tried," he said. "But I
can't."

"What do you mean you can't? Come on. Get going!"

"But, Mommy, I can't. There's no car in the garage!"

My mind was so full of details I had forgotten that the
car had been towed to the auto repair shop. My child was
right. He couldn't obey me. It was impossible.

There are impossible situations when we simply can't
obey. It's like trying to get into a car that isn't there. But
then there are some situations that only appear to be
impossible, and God asks us to believe and obey Him.
Jesus said to a disabled man, "Stretch out your hand"
(Matt. 12:13). The command seemed impossible and probably ridiculous to the man. However, when he decided to
obey the impossible command and to stretch out his hand,
he was immediately made whole. The man had looked for

help in the right place, from the right person. He listened to the directions, as ridiculous as they sounded, and then chose to follow them. The truth is, we all have a disability at one time or another, and we need the miraculous touch of God to make us whole. The seemingly impossible in our lives can be a place of victory if we will choose to obey God's commands.

WHAT COMMANDS MUST I OBEY?

If asked, "What are God's commandments?" most of us would respond, "Well, first there are the 'Thou shalt not's.' " Interestingly, when some people asked Jesus what they must do to please God, He said, "Believe in Him whom He sent" (John 6:29). Salvation starts with God's gift to us, not with our obedience to Him. All of our obedience to God without His gift of Jesus is meaningless. The appropriate response to someone who gives us a gift we cannot buy or cannot earn is to seek to please the giver. Above all else then, to please God, we must believe in Jesus and become one of God's children. We must acknowledge our disobedience through sin, recognize Christ died for those sins, and accept His free gift of salvation.

This is the initial step of obedience to God. Then Jesus also said that two commandments among "all the Law and the Prophets" are the greatest: "You shall love the LORD your God with all your heart, with all your soul, and with all your mind"; and "You shall love your neighbor as yourself" (Matt. 22:36–40).

I wondered what it meant to "love the LORD your God with all your heart, with all your soul, and with all your mind." What was the most important thing in my life? What did I spend most of my time and energy on? I examined how I spent the minutes of my day, what I spent my money on, and what I filled my mind with (what I watched on TV and what I read).

Picture a circle cut into several pie-shaped pieces. Each wedge can be filled with an aspect of your life: work, family, social life, finances, recreation, and so on. When you first become a Christian, it is natural to allow Jesus to fill one of the empty wedges. Placing Him in one of these spaces means He can have an influence on the two adjacent pieces, perhaps work and family. The other areas of your life are insulated from His influence because He is not in a position to touch them directly. Now picture, instead, an old-fashioned wagon wheel with spokes and a hub in the center. Fill in all the pie-shaped sections once again with aspects of your life. This time place Jesus in the center, in the hub. Now He has access to every area of your life.

The booklet *My Heart Christ's Home* by Robert Munger also illustrates this idea of giving Christ access to every area of our lives. God says that when we love Him and obey Him, He will help us remake our "home" into a place where Jesus feels welcome in every room (John 14:23). Jesus calls us to follow Him, to grow up, to change, and to become holy through the act of obedience. If any part of our lives is insulated from His influence, He is less than the Lord of our lives; we are not loving the Lord our God with all our hearts, with all our souls, and with all our minds.

When we reexamine the command linked with the promise "Trust in the LORD, and do good; . . . Delight yourself also in the LORD, and He shall give you the desires of your heart" (Ps. 37:3–4), we see that "delighting" is crucial to loving the Lord with all your heart. We are commanded first to do good and then to delight. We are promised the desires of our hearts. These desires will have been shaped by our good deeds and our enjoyment of God. The godly yearning of our souls will be satisfied, not necessarily the appetites of our bodies. The great Bible commentator Matthew Henry was asked, "What is the desire of the heart of a good person?" He said, "It is this: to know, and love, and live to God, to please Him and be pleased in Him."[3] I found that being pleased in Him was the contentment I experienced when I was doing what was right.

As we look at the second great commandment, to love your neighbor as yourself, we must take into account much of the discussion in chapter 4. This commandment implies that before you can love others, you must first love yourself. It is OK to love yourself because God values you. You are a valuable, precious, unrepeatable creation of God. You are worth loving, worth dying for, and worth changing. Though it is a reassurance to know God loves us so unconditionally, it is also a call to duty. We are commanded to love others as we love ourselves. I wasn't worried about this obligation until I realized that God valued my husband the same as He valued me. Was God commanding me to love someone who at that very moment I actually hated?

I soon discovered His answer was yes. In time, God Himself gave me love for my husband. In my own strength, it was one of those impossible situations. A benefit of obeying the command was the freedom I had from a life of bitterness and unforgiveness.

Your pain identifies you—your choices will direct you. The pain of a broken promise—someone else's disobedience—or your own disobedience may identify you. Even when we know why we should obey and even when we want to obey, we all will fail at times. Your pain can point you to your need for grace and the need to know God better, the One who never breaks any promise He has made.

> *Dear Lord, give me the courage to believe in Your promises and to trust You enough to obey. I want to benefit from all You have to give me. Help me place You in the center of all that I am and all that I do, no matter what it costs. In Jesus' name, Amen.*

WHILE YOU'RE CHOOSING TO GET SERIOUS WITH GOD, TAKE TIME TO CONSIDER...

1. What important promises to you have been broken? Why?
2. Which people can you trust? Why?
3. What promises have you chosen to break lately? Which have you been unable to keep?
4. What burdens are you carrying? Are they heavy or light?
5. What promises of God would you like to apply to your life?
6. What are some of your honest doubts about God's abilities and His timing?
7. Do you feel free to date? If you are dating, do you see the person as a lifelong partner?
8. What temptations are you facing?
9. Are you aware of a command God has asked you to obey? Are you willing?
10. What is the most important thing in your life? What do you spend most of your time and energy on?

11. Do you think it is possible to love your spouse as you love yourself?
12. In what areas of your life will it take courage to trust God and obey His commands? What are you willing to risk?

NOTES

1. Kurt De Haan, *How Does God Keep His Promises?* (Grand Rapids, Mich.: Radio Bible Class, 1989), p. 3.

2. Bob Burns and Tom Whiteman, *The Fresh Start Divorce Recovery Workbook* (Nashville: Oliver-Nelson, 1992), pp. 74–75.

3. Matthew Henry, *Commentary on the Whole Bible* (Grand Rapids, Mich.: Zondervan, 1961), p. 613.

CHAPTER SEVEN

Choose to Balance Your Life

I looked down, very far down from the chairlift. *How did I ever get myself into this? If I break a leg, who will take care of my kids? They need me; I'm all they have now.*

I turned to the young woman sitting next to me with well-worn boots and skis, and I said, "I bet you've done this before."

"Every day I can," she replied. "I work at the lodge. I moved here just so I could ski on my off hours. How about you?"

"I took classes this morning and skied down the bunny slope three times. I've only been on a ski lift once before, and that was on a sunny day years ago with my parents."

"I remember when I first learned how to ski. I bet you're having a ball."

"To be honest," I swallowed hard and looked straight ahead, "I'm really scared. I don't like heights."

"You'll get used to it. It's all part of the thrill."

"Maybe I'm just too old for a thrill. Say . . . after I get to the top," I paused and made the mistake of looking down, "if I decide I don't want to ski down . . . where do I catch a lift to ride down?"

"Oh, you can't do that," she chuckled. "They never allow anyone to ride down the lift."

"Never? You're kidding me, right?"

"No, I'm really serious."

All I knew to do then was pray, "Oh, Lord, You'll have to get me out of this one. I'm scared! I don't know what the instructor was thinking when she suggested I do this. I'm not prepared. This seems impossible."

It all seemed like a good idea last month when my friend Cindy called long distance. "Hey, Jan, have you made plans for Thanksgiving yet?" she asked.

"Can't say as I have," I replied. "There have been a few changes around here, you know. Things will be different this year."

I had just moved to a new town. My parents lived far away, and the children would spend Thanksgiving for the first time at their father's new house. *Thanksgiving is supposed to be a family time. What kind of a mom doesn't even eat turkey with her kids? This isn't how I had pictured my holidays as a parent.*

I was finally able to get out, "Maybe I'll invite some people over to my place." *But who would I invite? Another family, with a dad? Couples? Only single people? I hardly know anyone to invite anyway . . . I've never been so lonely in all my life.*

My attention came back to Cindy as she said, "I called to tell you about a singles conference through Campus

Crusade for Christ in Keystone, Colorado. Unfortunately, I can't go this year, but I really think you'd enjoy it. I'll send you the info, OK?"

"OK," I said. "Thanks a lot. Bye." I caught her just before she hung up, "Hey, wait a minute. Do I honestly qualify? You know my divorce isn't final yet." I hesitated a moment before adding, "But I am lonely. Is that 'single' enough?"

"Sure! I met several separated people there when I went last year. The purpose of the conference is to encourage people to put their hope in the Lord, not in a mate. A separated person can benefit from that as much as anyone else—maybe more."

Now here I was at the singles retreat, on top of the mountain on my own. Trying desperately to maintain my balance, I maneuvered my way off the ski lift without a fall. It was snowing, and a gust of freezing wind hit my face. With every ounce of strength and concentration I had, I followed the green flags down the first slope. Fifty feet from the bottom, I lost my balance and discovered what it was like to "bottom ski." I plowed smack into a snowbank.

"What should I do now?" I asked a passerby, skis cradled on his shoulder.

Without offering to help me up, he said, "I guess you can stay there forever . . . or get up and get going where you were headed."

WHERE WAS I HEADING?

So many things in my life were changing. I had lost my job and sold my house. Now I needed a new doctor, a new church, a new job, a new house, and new friends, but I had less time, less money, and less strength to meet those decisions and demands. Each night as I prepared for bed I wondered what the next day would bring.

I had moved from southern California to a small town on the central coast of California. Often from our living room I could see boats in the vast open sea. One day I glanced out the window to see a small boat bobbing up and down all alone in the rough waves. *I feel just like that boat. My anchor is gone, and my mooring has disappeared. The waves are rough, and I'm being tossed to and fro. What I thought was secure and predictable has been torn away by this storm of separation. Will I always feel like I don't fit in, or will I someday find a comfortable place in society? Will I always feel so lonely, or will I someday find relief?*

Loneliness and depression, though two different emotions, are linked. Both are a normal part of the grieving process, as discussed in chapter 3. Loneliness usually *generates pressure to change*; sometimes it pushes us to *any* activity that offers hope for relief. Believing there are solutions to our problems, we keep experimenting, sometimes foolishly or even dangerously. Depression usually *resists change*; it numbs the thinking and inhibits the ability to take action. Believing there is no solution to the pain, a depressed person often wants to stay at home, full of self-pity.

You can overcome the loneliness brought about by change and loss in your life when you recognize two things. First, since you are capable of action, you are to some extent personally responsible to find relief from your loneliness. Second, since God is with you, you really are never alone. Once God has given you spiritual relief from the anguish of loneliness, you need never fear being lonely again. You needn't wait for someone else to do something for you. You will benefit from the pain of your loneliness if you choose to get up, brush yourself off, and do what it takes to get down the mountain.

WHY AM I SO STRESSED OUT?

A booklet published by the Hope Heart Institute states, "When we allow too much change into our lives at one time, stress increases and illness is the typical result."[1] No wonder separation and divorce are second only to the death of a spouse as the leading cause of stress in one's life. Change is inevitable during separation—lots of it! You feel stress because any change places demands upon your energy for coping and adapting.

Some separated people feel overwhelmed and wish for a return to the way things were. I saw this happen to a friend of mine who had been married to an alcoholic who physically abused her and the children. One day Teresa said to me, "I don't want things to change anymore. Maybe things weren't really as bad as I thought." At the time, I was surprised that she felt that the severe problems of her marriage were more bearable than the changes she faced. Now I'm not surprised. Not many of us enjoy change that involves replacing the predictable (even if it's not healthy) with the unpredictable.

Some changes in our lives are the result of a deliberate choice on our part: "I'm going back to school to get my degree"; "It's time to stay home and have a family"; "We'd like to adopt another child"; "Let's try to sell this house and start looking for a bigger one"; "Our marriage is over; I'm moving out." Other changes are forced upon us by someone else, a situation, or circumstances: "We're losing money; everyone in the company must take a cut in pay"; "The owner of your rental house wants to sell; you'll have to move"; "I made a bad business decision; you'll have to help out and go back to work"; "I'm in love with someone else; you'll have to sign these divorce papers."

Separation brings a change in your responsibilities and in your identity. Some results of the changes are easy for others to see: new standard of living, new home, new job, new activities, new social standing, and new friends. The change in your relationships may result in the loss of companionship, causing loneliness, which may not be as easy for others to see or understand.

The change in your responsibilities affects almost every area of daily living. To become solely responsible for your household causes stress; even if you are now living alone, you are assuming duties that you once shared. If you are suddenly a single parent, you have increased household duties, and you must meet the physical and emotional needs of your children. You are single-handedly facing situations that demand quick, if not immediate, decisions. Sometimes the hurried decisions will have long-term effects on you or your children. You need to find answers to many questions: Should I file for divorce right away? Where should I live? Can I afford it? How can I make enough money to support two households? Should I get a job? Should I quit my job? Who will care for the kids when I'm not at home?

I was not prepared for the changes in my social identity when I was separated. Even going to the doctor's office with my child turned out to be a trial.

"As soon as you complete this form, the doctor will see your daughter," the medical secretary said, handing me a clipboard.

I studied the boxes demanding a check mark: "Single"; "Married"; "Divorced." *I'm not divorced yet . . . I feel single . . . I need my husband's help to pay this bill . . . I guess the only one to check is "Married."*

I continued and entered "Father's name" where it was requested. Then I faced more boxes: "Father lives in home"; "Father lives outside of home." As I got ready to mark the box "Father lives outside of home," I thought, *What kind of person is married to someone who doesn't live in the home?* I went back and erased my check mark in the "Married" box and squeezed "Separated" between the boxes. *Next time I come here, will I be checking off the "Divorced" box? If I am divorced by then, I think I would rather check "Single." But how would I explain the children? What am I anyway?*

The next day I prepared a birthday card to send to my mother-in-law. As I began writing, "Dear Mom," I thought, *Who am I to her? I'm her daughter-in-law because I married her son. Maybe I should sign, "Love, your separated daughter-in-law"? How much longer will I be her daughter-in-law? Does she care? Will I offend her?*

Our social standing defines us and provides a structure for our actions and activities. The loss of social identity brings confusion and increases stress. Are you wondering how you fit in as a separated family? Do any of these thoughts seem familiar? *I'm a family and so I should keep doing family things. The problem is, part of the family is missing.* Or *A lot has changed. I'm trying to make the best of it, but even if I tried to go on a family vacation, I couldn't afford it now as a single parent.* Or *We've tried to do the same things as always on holidays. But it's not the same; we don't have the same family anymore.*

Some days I had a positive attitude and could embrace change. Other days I was afraid and was relieved simply to have made it through the day. Review the "Survival Tips" at the end of chapter 3, but label them now as "Stress Busters." I hope you can find something there that will help you get through another day, week, or month of changes.

WHAT IS LONELINESS?

My separation changed my social life greatly. I was unprepared for the great sense of loneliness I felt within months after my separation. There had always been someone in my life with whom I could share intimately. I had moved from my family to a college roommate and then directly to a marriage partner. I had always been able to look forward to collapsing on the couch at the end of the day (grubs and all), there to share my thoughts, feelings, and struggles with someone. During my separation, when my needs seemed the greatest, I longed for the companionship I had always known. I could get through my day, but I dreaded the evening. I feared the silence that came after I put the children to bed. The still house brought the reminder that no one was waiting to hear about my day: No one cared how I felt. I would crawl into an empty bed, anxious for sleep to shut out the loneliness.

Why is it that some people can be alone but not be lonely? Or why is it that some people can be in the midst of a crowd of people but ache with loneliness? Loneliness is something more than the absence or presence of people. God said, "It is not good that man should be alone; I will make him a helper comparable to him" (Gen. 2:18). He created us social beings, capable of giving and receiving love through marriage and other relationships. Loneliness comes when we feel isolated from those relationships God intended us to have with Himself and others.

I do not believe we must be lonely because we are solitary. Granted, solitary confinement is a punishment, but solitude can also be a welcomed physical separation from people that offers a positive, energizing experience. Jesus made deliberate choices to be alone in order to have communion with His Father (Mark 1:35). We are instructed to do the same. If we want to stay in touch with God, we must be ready, willing, and able to hear His voice. Solitude gives us an opportunity to listen and be personally renewed and be equipped to respond to the needs of others. Times of solitude are essential to recharge some people in order to face the stress in their lives. Additionally, solitude is essential for all of us who seek to "regain heaven's perspective on the mysteries of life."[2]

I believe isolation is the root of loneliness. Isolation is not merely physical separation from others, as the dictionary might suggest. To cause loneliness, the separation must involve emotional, social, or spiritual separation/isolation. The need for emotional intimacy can be met by a marriage partner or a family member or a best friend. The need can be met by several people throughout a lifetime. These relationships provide security; you know there is someone you can count on. You feel accepted for who you are. If your primary emotional relationship was with your spouse, separation will certainly result in loneliness. However, some people don't have their emotional needs met in the marriage relationship. My friend Beverly told me, "I was never more lonely than when I was married. I still don't know if he ever loved me."

If you are lonely and desire an emotional relationship, you might want to search out a new friend. Beverly's separation allowed her to develop a deeper companionship with her best friend, Suzy. I do offer a word of warning here: Select with caution who you will allow to meet your emotional need during this uncertain time of separation. In the last chapter, you saw what happened to me when I filled that desire too quickly with a member of the oppo-site sex.

The need for social relationships is often met by a pro-fession, children, or social organizations. Separation can disrupt the established network. We are uncomfortable with our former associates, or they are uncomfortable with us. Nonetheless, we continue to need to be a part of a community, to feel we are making a contribution to the world beyond ourselves. We need to be connected with people who share our interests and beliefs, who give us a sense of purpose and belonging. If you need a change, don't drop out totally; look around, and try something new: Everything from the Red Cross to the Turtle Club to the AIDS Awareness Task Force can meet this need. It is important to continue (or to begin) developing satisfying social relationships in church. Here people are meant to overcome isolation by encouraging one another and work-ing together. If we aren't involved in the lives of others through social relationships, no matter where that is, we will feel left out, isolated and lonely.

Spiritual loneliness is variously described as a vacuum, a void, or a hole inside us that we intuitively know only God can fill. If at one time we had an active and warm relationship with God, our loneliness is especially notice-able. Just by the tone of her voice I knew my friend Heidi was struggling. We were talking on the phone when she said, "God seems so distant right now. I know why, too. I've heard the saying, 'If God seems far away, guess who moved?' Well, I know who moved. I haven't been obedi-ent lately. I know whatever God has to teach me is going to take time . . . but sometimes it's just so hard to wait and do things His way." Our greatest need is to be in a right relationship with God. We must not ignore any signs that indicate something is wrong. Even if our emotional and social needs are being met, there will always be a spiritual vacuum if we don't stay in touch with God.

WHO AM I?

Changes came fast and furious during my separation. As I said before, at times I was prepared, and I handled them well. Other times I failed miserably. Sometimes I relished the challenge of it all. Other times I felt pressured and overwhelmed by stress. Why was it so important for me to have closure and end the period of separation once and for all, one way or the other? Closure seemed unimportant to my husband. Why did I sense such deep loneliness and want to surround myself with other people? Companionship seemed unimportant to my husband. He actually seemed to enjoy being alone. I gradually learned, and more important accepted, the truth that my husband and I had different approaches to life. During our marriage, I knew he saw things differently, but I never had taken the time to find out why. Now I needed to know.

I hope this little illustration will give you some insight into one of the lessons I learned. A small swallow, having been knocked about by our playful dog, lay helpless on the grass in our backyard. When my son noticed the bird, he went outside to rescue "the little birdie." He frightened it as he approached. With great effort, on one chewed wing, the bird flew to a nearby fence.

"Mommy, come outside quick! I want to show you something. Look, I've taught the bird to fly!"

It was true that the bird had flown, but it had nothing to do with my son's abilities or teaching skills. He had no flying skills, and he certainly couldn't teach a bird to fly. Those were not skills God had given him.

I spent years of my life believing I was teaching birds to

fly. I imagined God had given me certain abilities, which He definitely had not. For instance, I was not capable of remaking my husband into my image. I really didn't know what was best for him, even though I thought I did. He may have altered his behavior (flown to the nearby fence) but not because of my ability or teaching skill. He, like the bird, was scared off. I had been wasting my time and energy.

I read a lot of books and studied many different models that sought to explain why we do what we do. I found the most understandable explanation in the book *Please Understand Me* by David Keirsey and Marilyn Bates.[3] I value this model because it specifically addresses the issues of aloneness and change. It is also a guilt reliever because no one type is portrayed as right or wrong—just different. Everyone ends up a winner. When I share these ideas, I get comments like, "I never wanted to go out with my husband in crowds. Now that I understand why I'm more uncomfortable than he is, I don't feel so guilty anymore." Or "I always got so frustrated when my husband would suggest we go on a picnic instead of working on our 'to-do' list. Now that I understand why I want to stick to a work plan and why he so easily dismisses it for playtime, I don't feel so angry with him anymore."

When I clearly understood my God-given preferences, I experienced balance between my skills, interests, and tendencies. With that new balance came greater development of my abilities and thus increased achievements because I was freed to live up to my potential. I desired to understand the special and unique characteristics God had built into other people, too. I needed to learn not to judge or expect everyone to act as I thought best. As I truly began to appreciate the value of individuality, I was freed to accept others more for who God had created them to be than for who I could force them to be.

WHAT CAN I DO ABOUT MY LONELINESS?

No one else can solve your problem of loneliness. If you want to find relief, you must take the initiative. Even though your natural tendency may not be to surround yourself with people, most of us are looking for some social contact. If you're unsure, begin by placing yourself in safe places where you can enjoy a sense of connection. You may need to force yourself to make a plan to get where you know you need to go. In the Disney movie *Alice in Wonderland*, the Cheshire cat points out to Alice that if she doesn't know where she wants to go, it doesn't matter which road she follows—any road will take her there. Make a plan and follow the road to your unfinished daydreams. I took quilting and photography classes—they were things I had always wanted to do but somehow had never gotten around to. Judy, a friend of mine, took a skydiving class and then made the big jump on her fortieth birthday. She was energized even though the cost of her dream included a doctor's bill for a broken ankle, caused by a bad landing!

On a more down-to-earth level, try attending a workshop for separated people.[4] Make a conscious decision to become involved at your church, join a small group study, sing in the choir, become a committee member, get to know the people you work with, and attend work-related social functions.

Of course, being busy and active or just being around people isn't always the answer to loneliness. What about the introvert who is lonely in a crowded room? I believe the necessary ingredient is attitude. When you are willing to extend yourself to meet the needs of others and stop looking for someone to meet your needs, you are ready to be a friend. That's what companionship is all about. Maybe this is the time to encourage someone, even someone you don't usually call, with a phone call. Write a letter of encouragement to your pastor, baby-sitter, or parents. When you are willing to give and to involve yourself in the lives of others, you offset your selfish, inward-looking tendency to feel sorry for yourself. Loving others is an action that promotes wholeness and balance in your life. No matter what your personality type, you can improve your social life by learning to love the way God does: unselfishly, mercifully, and righteously.

The way I satisfied my need for emotional involvement and companionship while I was separated may not fit your circumstances or your preferences. You need to look around at options that suit you. Perhaps your present loneliness has made you realize that your marriage had many benefits. If both you and your partner are willing to take the necessary steps to seek reconciliation, this may be the time to admit your desire for renewed intimacy with your spouse.

I'm very grateful for two special people I could share my life with during the years I was separated. You've heard about Bruce, but not Sarah. She and I were moms who were separated. We missed the companionship of our husbands. As our relationship grew, we spoke together daily, either face-to-face or on the phone. We shared many meals together, with kids and without kids. We both missed having someone to make memories with, so we decided to make some together. We had corned beef, cabbage, and soda bread every St. Patrick's Day. At Christmas we made candy houses with our children and followed the "ordeal" with a lasagna dinner. We even took a half-day deep-sea fishing trip to try our hands at something new. We shared our burdens, prayed together, and knew we could count on each other. We struggled together and laughed together. One of the notes she wrote to me said, "We will be better people for 'it' [meaning our separations] and will never become complacent with contentment. May we forever have caviar tastes on our peanut butter budgets." At one point we considered sharing a house to help with expenses. We decided against it, however, when we realized the total kid count of five would add even more stress to our already stricken lives. In both relationships, with Bruce and with Sarah, I took a risk to be vulnerable. I risked being hurt again. Unless you are willing to take such risks, your need for an intimate emotional relationship may never be met.

My friend Cindy, who had invited me to the singles conference, had never been married, yet she told me she wasn't lonely. Her life was in balance socially, personally, and especially spiritually. I had taken so much for granted until my life started to fall apart. I had never appreciated God's constant companionship. I didn't know that my greatest relationship need was spiritual, not social or emotional. It took the pain of loneliness to show me that I needed, beyond anything else, to be in a right relationship with God. We read in the Bible that even Jesus was lonely. He overcame His loneliness because He knew the truth, that actually He was not alone. He said to His disciples, "[You] will leave Me alone. Yet I am not alone, because the Father is with Me" (John 16:32). There was no one on earth Jesus could count on; He'd been rejected and despised; He felt no one cared for Him. Yet He did not despair, for He knew He wasn't isolated: He had a relationship with God, His Father.

God is available for us, too. We will never be alone if we respond by faith to His offer of a relationship through Jesus Christ. So, where is God when we're lonely? He assures us that He is always with us. Although everything around you might be changing, God will not change (Mal. 3:6) or leave you or forsake you (Heb. 13:5). He promised! God never creates a need in us that He cannot fill, but He requires us to get involved in the process.

I wanted my daughter to be happy in our new home. I knew she needed friends, and I knew she'd find them at school. At first she was not very willing to go along with the plan. "But I don't want to go to my new school today," she said. "I don't know anybody."

"I'm sorry, dear, but you have no choice. You're going."

At the end of the day she burst through the door and kissed me. Her first words were, "I'm so glad you made me go. I got to paint, play puzzles, and sing. Oh, and I met a new friend. Can she come over to play today?"

Perhaps you feel forced by others, including God, to face change or to do something you don't want to do. After a time, with heightened awareness, you might find yourself saying, "I'm so glad you made me go."

Your pain identifies you—your choices will direct you. There are times we have no choice and must deal with painful changes. The pain of loneliness may identify you right now. You may feel your life is out of balance. If you choose to deny your responsibility and blame others for your condition, hope for relief is slim. In contrast, if you choose to love others unselfishly, understanding personality differences rather than condemning them, you will reestablish the emotional and social balance in your life. Your fundamental need is to have a balanced relationship with God Himself. Under His care, change can be your ally.

> *Dear Lord, I desire to become all that You intended. Give me the strength to take the risks necessary to meet the needs You created in me. I want to know, as never before, that I am not alone. Help me to place my relationship with You above all others, that I might experience that reality. In Jesus' name, Amen.*

WHILE YOU'RE CHOOSING TO BALANCE YOUR LIFE, TAKE TIME TO CONSIDER . . .

1. What changes are you facing? Are they of your choosing or of circumstance?
2. How do you feel you are handling the changes? Are you stressed? Overwhelmed? Challenged? Excited? Relieved?
3. What responsibilities have changed in your life?
4. Do you find it hard to fit in?
5. Are you energized by people or by solitude?
6. When do you experience loneliness?
7. Do you believe you are responsible to find relief for your loneliness? Do you have a plan?
8. When you've followed a past plan, have you been pleased with the results?
9 What do you need to know or feel in order to make a decision?
10. Was your need for an intimate emotional relationship met in your marriage? Is that need being met now?

11. Do you feel isolated and cut off from social relationships? What do you need to do to meet your need?
12. Do you have a spiritual vacuum? What must you do to set things right?

NOTES

1. "Taking Charge of Life's Changes," *Adapting to Stress: Health-trac—Start Taking Charge* (Seattle: The Hope Heart Institute, 1989), pp. 6–7.

2. J. Oswald Sanders, *Lonely But Never Alone* (Grand Rapids, Mich.: Radio Bible Class, 1991), p. 18.

3. David Keirsey and Marilyn Bates, *Please Understand Me* (Del Mar, Calif.: Prometheus Nemesis Books, 1978), p. 14.

4. Fresh Start Seminars, Inc., is a help seminar for divorced and separated persons that originated in 1980 at the Church of the Saviour in Wayne, Pennsylvania. Since that time, Fresh Start has grown into a ministry that offers weekend seminars to churches through the eastern and southern parts of the country. For more information about Fresh Start, write Fresh Start Seminars, Inc., 63 Chestnut Road, Paoli, Pennsylvania 19301. Or call 1-800-882-2799.

CHAPTER EIGHT

Choose to Stay in Touch with God

"I don't understand why he doesn't answer," I said to my mom. "Where could he be? He never leaves for work this early." I had tried calling my husband several times since arriving at my parents' house. *What's wrong?*

I waited anxiously until noon, hoping he would call me. There was so much I needed to talk to him about. I finally decided to call his office, only to discover he had called in sick for the day. *Was he really sick? Was he staying with someone else? Had he gone to see the pastor as he'd promised?*

Early the next morning I tried our number once again. The busy signal I heard brought hope—hope that someone was finally home and I might soon know what had happened. My heart raced when I finally heard the normal ringing tone.

"Hello."

"Oh, honey," I said. "I can't believe I finally reached you! I've been trying for days. It's so nice to hear your voice!"

"It's no wonder you couldn't reach me. Last night I went to use the phone, and I discovered the ringer was turned off!"

After a brief conversation, I hung up, relieved and frustrated. *All this time I've been imagining the worst. What a dummy! I turned off that ringer the last time I was sleeping during the day. I guess I had so much on my mind getting ready to come here I never thought to turn it back on.* Suddenly, I remembered the phone in the den. *He should have heard that one ring even if the other phone was turned off.*

When I arrived home, I went directly to the den to confirm my renewed suspicions. Looking behind the overstuffed chair, I saw the phone plug lying on the floor. I called out to my husband, "I wonder how the phone got unplugged in here?"

Our three-year-old came running into the den. I asked her, "Did you do something with the phone, honey?"

"I was just seeing how it went 'in and out . . . out and in' before we went on the airplane to Nannie's. It's fun!"

My husband walked into the den in time to hear our daughter's explanation. "Come to think of it," he paused, "I never did hear that phone ring while you were gone."

WHY COMMUNICATE?

I had been anxious to communicate directly with my husband in order to find out what was going on. He had been content to communicate later when he was ready—on his own terms and not before. I realized then, more than ever, how important communication is to a relationship. I knew that no matter what happened to my marriage, I wanted to develop my relationship with God. I didn't want to be cut off from Him as I had been from my husband.

I was eager to talk with my husband because I needed reassurance; in fact, I was hounding him. God is eager to talk with us, not because He needs reassurance but because He has important things to tell us. Unfortunately, we can be so busy and involved, even doing good things at church, that our ringer is turned off and we miss His call. If we have never entered into a relationship with God through Jesus, we might miss the call because we're completely unplugged.

God communicates on His terms (just like my husband), yet He is ready and available anytime and any place to talk to us (unlike my husband). God's line is never busy. He communicates with us through prayer, through the Holy Bible (His Word), and through the church (the body of Christ). He does this by filling us with the Holy Spirit who helps us pray, quickens our minds as we read the Bible, and coordinates our work in the church (see Rom. 8:26; John 14:26; 1 Cor. 12:3–31).

A friend admitted to me, "I don't think I will like praying, reading the Bible, or going to church, but . . . I really want to be a Christian. Will I have to do those things?" I did my best to explain that if we make a decision to have a relationship with Christ, prayer, Bible study, and fellowship are essential for maintaining that relationship. It may take time and effort to stay in touch with God, but this communion is as critical to our spiritual well-being as breathing is to our physical well-being. Besides, they are commands of God (1 Thess. 5:17; 2 Tim. 2:15; Heb. 10:25). If we don't feel like it, obedience to God should motivate us to incorporate these disciplines into our lives. They will change us and help us to know God Himself.

The result will be a faith to call our own—one we can't help sharing with others.

WHY IS IT SO HARD TO PRAY?

I had always thought I needed to pray to let God know what I wanted so that He could carry out His job. I figured that His job was to listen to my requests and then to grant my wishes like a genie in the sky. Since I rarely received what I asked for, I assumed my prayers were ineffectual or God was ineffective. Frustration and weariness summed up my relationship with Him since prayer determines the quality of most relationships with God. My friend Chris didn't have a quality relationship, either, because he avoided prayer as much as possible. He reasoned, "Since God's all-knowing, He certainly doesn't need me to inform Him of anything. Why pray at all?"

I remember feeling confused like Elizabeth. Over the phone one night she said to me, "I feel so desperate. I talk to God all the time because I need Him so much now, but I really don't know what to pray for anymore. Should I ask for my marriage to be healed? I'm not sure if I really want my marriage to succeed . . . or if I just don't want to fail. How should I pray?"

We know God has answered our prayers when we see results. He responds by speaking to us through His words found in the Bible, through the working of the Holy Spirit in our lives, or through circumstances or other people. The evidence of His answer is not always external or physical. Sometimes the evidence is internal and heartfelt—calmness, peace, strength, new understanding, or boldness. When we are in proper relationship with God, He will hear and answer our prayers (Ps. 66:19). He answers yes, no, or wait. When God says, "Wait," it's not because He's indifferent. His great love for us includes a desire to deepen and develop our faith in Him.[1] Often He knows that waiting is the only way to accomplish this work. However, the Bible makes it clear that such things as unconfessed sin (Ps. 66:18; Prov. 28:9; Isa. 1:15), pride (Job 35:12–13; Matt. 6:5, 7), wrong motives (James 4:3), and doubt (James 1:6–7) disturb our relationship with God and can render our prayers ineffective. Until we turn away from our error, thus allowing God to restore our relationship we may not receive any answer to our prayers.

If we approach prayer wanting God to do something *for* us, we will miss God's purpose for prayer altogether. Oswald Chambers said, "We look upon prayer as a means of getting things for ourselves; the Bible idea of prayer is that we may get to know God Himself."[2] God rarely does something *for* us unless He does something *in* us as well. If our goal as Christians is to know Christ more completely (Phil. 3:10), prayer will help us to accomplish that goal. Dr. Lloyd Ogilvie said, "Successful prayer is not measured by how much we get from God, but how much of Him gets into us."[3]

HOW SHOULD I PRAY?

Our view of God is distorted when we focus our attention on ourselves and our needs or problems rather than on God Himself. As we seek to manipulate Him, prayer becomes "an attempt to move God over to our point of view—to get God to do what we want done—to use Him as a means to our end. In prayer we ought to seek to discover God's point of view and how, when, and where He wants us to move and live . . . and obey."[4] If we can choose to put God in the driver's seat and our needs in the backseat, we can begin to pray from God's perspective rather than our own. When we surrender ourselves and are humble, we can honestly pray as Jesus taught us to pray, "Your will be done" (Matt. 6:10).

That is the attitude God responds to, whether the prayer is offered in public or in private, on a park bench or on a carpeted floor. Prayer is the great privilege of communicating with God intimately—anytime, any place, and in any manner. In a group (church, Bible study group, family and friends, and so on), we have the special promise of Jesus that He will be right there with even two or three who are gathered in His name; if we agree on anything, it will be done (Matt. 18:19–20). However, we are warned against showy public prayers. Jesus instructs us to enter into an inner chamber and shut the door to pray to God in secret; then God will reward us (Matt. 6:6). We are told, "Pray without ceasing" (1 Thess. 5:17), not, "Thou shalt not stand at the kitchen sink and pray; thou shalt kneel in a position of reverence." To me that means, "Go ahead and pray while you're at the kitchen sink, in the shower, your car, your office, or wherever."

Many years ago I learned the word ACTS to help me remember the elements of an effective prayer life. I remember thinking that unless I went through this entire process every time I prayed, God would be unhappy with me and, therefore, would not hear my prayers. I now believe He hears my quick plea for help from the kitchen sink as clearly as He hears my plea after thirty minutes of organized prayer. However, you will pray more effectively if you keep these principles in mind.

Adoration

Adoration is the praise we offer to God.

You are worthy, O Lord,

To receive glory and honor and power;
For You created all things,
And by Your will they exist and were created (Rev.
   4:11).

It is His will for us that we continuously praise Him for who He is (Pss. 34:1; 50:23; Isa. 43:21). Our praise brings Him pleasure (Ps. 92:1) because it strengthens the bond of love between God and His people. The act of praise itself helps us look beyond a problem (such as separation, unemployment, or anger) and recognize the Source of healing: "Praise is the spark plug of faith."[5] It "is the detergent which purifies faith and purges doubt from the heart. The secret of faith without doubt is praise, triumphant praise, continuous praise, praise that is a way of life. This is the solution to the problem of a living faith and successful prayer."[6] Reading psalms silently or aloud helps me praise God. Do whatever turns your thoughts to the wonder of who God is.

Confession

Confession is agreement with God about our sin. It is an admission of our inability to be in proper relationship with Him except through forgiveness and the cleansing power of the blood of Christ (Col. 1:13–14). First, we are to admit our sin and repent (choose to turn from our sinful way to go God's way; Ps. 51:3–4; Acts 2:38). Next, we are to ask forgiveness (2 Cor. 7:9–10), and finally, believe that God has restored us. Jesus' disciple John wrote, "If we confess our sins, He is faithful and just to forgive us our sins and to cleanse us from all unrighteousness" (1 John 1:9). God's answer is always yes to this prayer.

We need to keep short accounts with God. As we become more sensitive to our sins, the Holy Spirit may show us a need to forgive others or to seek forgiveness from others. When we confess what we couldn't do and what we didn't do—the if only's in our lives—we can stop looking back at the past and move forward in a new direction.

Thanksgiving

Thanksgiving shows gratitude. We should thank God for what He does, who He is, and what He makes of us. We are instructed to give thanks in everything, but especially for His work in creation and for His redemption (1 Thess. 5:18; Ps. 100; Rev. 4:11; 5:9). In the midst of the agony of separation it's hard to be thankful because we usually don't believe we deserve the pain we are experiencing or we think we are entitled to special treatment because we are one of God's chosen. It might not feel natural to be thankful in a difficult situation, but it is a skill God will help us develop. To be thankful while we wait for God's answers, we need humility and the change in perspective it brings. Ben Patterson in his book *Waiting* suggests, "Humility comes from being very clear on the fact that God is God and we are merely his creatures. Humility recognizes that we exist for God's sake, not he for ours. Only the humble know they have no demands they can lay on God and his world."[7]

Supplication

Supplication is a request made on behalf of ourselves and others. Jesus encouraged us to do so when He said, "Ask, and it will be given to you; seek, and you will find; knock, and it will be opened to you" (Matt. 7:7). It's too bad that we are so often shortsighted, asking for physical needs but excluding spiritual ones. You can use Scripture to help you pray for yourself and others. Try using your or another's name as you read Ephesians 1:17–19 as a prayer. God wants all of His creation to comprehend the love of Christ (Eph. 3:14–17) and have His power at work in their lives (Eph. 1:17–19). We are to ask for forgiveness and wisdom that we may be in the center of God's will (1 John 1:9; James 1:5). He responds to prayers made by faith and in the name of Jesus because they reflect His will (1 John 3:22; James 1:6; John 14:13). We are to pray for spiritual leaders (Col. 4:3), political authorities (1 Tim. 2:1–3), family and friends that God puts on our hearts (Eph. 6:18), and even our enemies (that may mean the "other" woman or the "other" man; Matt. 5:44).

Someone observed, "When we pray, we often concentrate on the gifts in God's hand and ignore the hand of God Himself."[8] God does give good gifts and satisfy our needs, but "those who are merely satisfied with the trinkets in the Father's hand miss the best reward of prayer—the reward of communicating and communing with the God of the universe."[9]

WHY IS IT SO HARD TO STUDY THE BIBLE?

I had always thought Bible study was the minister's job. The minister had gone to seminary to learn Hebrew and Greek and the historical facts to make sense of it all. I figured the minister's job was to study hard to know what God said in order to inform me on Sunday mornings (and maybe even Wednesday nights). I reasoned that since I was untrained, personal Bible study was a waste of my time. Joe admitted at a seminar, "I hardly ever read the Bible because I just don't understand the words. The only Bible I have is the one my aunt gave me years ago. I think she forgot I don't speak with thees and thous."

As English-speaking Christians, we are privileged to have available to us a variety of *translations, revisions,* and *paraphrased versions* of the Bible. *New translations* are not based on previous versions. The translators start from scratch, using the best available manuscripts and information and different interpretive styles or goals. They strive to understandably translate the original words, as much as possible, literally and exactly into English. *English revisions* alter established translations by incorporating up-to-date knowledge of the original text and changes in English speech. The King James Version has had five major revisions: 1629, 1638, 1762, 1769, and 1983. *Paraphrased versions* strive to express the meaning of the original words in basic contemporary English. Most of the versions we enjoy today have been produced since 1960: the New English Bible (NEB), the New International Version (NIV), the New American Standard Bible (NASB), the Living Bible (TLB), and the New King James Version (NKJV). If you aren't sure which version is best for you, go to a Bible bookstore and make some comparisons. Your church may suggest the use of a particular translation. It is important to have a Bible you can understand and feel comfortable using; otherwise, you'll wonder as Joe did why you should bother opening it.

"The greatest purpose of the written Word of God, the Bible, is to reveal the living Word of God, the Lord Jesus Christ,"[10] but some people associate this purpose with boredom and repetition. Judy said, "I was born and raised in the church. I don't doubt the Bible is God's Word, but I've heard every Bible story a hundred times. Tell me, how many ways can you apply the story of the good Samaritan?" Because some people think they know what the Bible is supposed to say, they often miss what it actually says. In point of fact, the Holy Spirit will continually use Scripture to teach us, answer questions, and change our lives (Eph. 3:14–21).

We should study the Bible because God is its author: "The Bible is God's Book. Although it was written by men like Moses and Luke and Paul, it is the self-revelation of God. He is the Author behind the authors. And what He says reflects who He is."[11] Even if you doubt that the Bible is the inspired Word of God, you can still benefit from studying it because "faith comes by hearing, and hearing by the word of God" (Rom. 10:17). One of the best ways to rid yourself of doubt is to start reading it and to agree to put into practice any truth you find there. If doubt about its authenticity continues to bother you, there are many books on the subject. A good one is *A Ready Defense* by Josh McDowell.

If we think we can get to know who God is by occasionally reading a verse or by listening to a sermon on Sunday, we will be disappointed. As we study for ourselves the written Word of God, He will speak to us, and our faith will grow, causing us to be more like Him.

HOW SHOULD I STUDY THE BIBLE?

The Bible can reveal God's answers to our prayers (Prov. 4:20–22; Heb. 4:12). Therefore, we should want to read the Scriptures. The Bible reveals who God is by telling us what He says and how He dealt with men and women of the past in every imaginable circumstance (Deut. 32:7; 1 Pet. 1:23). Therefore, we should want to read the Scriptures so we can know His concerns and judgments today. The Bible reveals God's plans for the future. Therefore, we should want to read the Scriptures so we'll know how to live today in preparation for the world to come. The Bible reveals God's love relationship with His creation through the life of Jesus Christ (John 3:16). Therefore, we should want to read the Scriptures so we might believe in Jesus and have the kind of faith that brings abundant and everlasting life (John 20:31). The Bible puts us in direct communication with God: It convicts (Neh. 8:9), corrects (Ps. 17:4), cleanses (Ps. 119:9), confirms truth in our hearts (John 8:31), instructs (Col. 3:16), equips (Prov. 22:21), and brings peace and freedom (Col. 3:15; John 8:32).

Bible study takes place in two settings. Both are valuable. The private setting enhances individual Bible study. It should involve a quiet devotional time with God as well as a time of in-depth study using one of several Bible study methods or a Bible study guide. The other setting for Bible study is with others: your family, church members, friends, and so on. Usually, these studies are structured to include both instructional and devotional times, which encourage friendships through shared knowledge and experience as well as communication with God.

You will find it helpful to have available various reference books, especially when you do in-depth studies. Apart from your understandable, easy-to-read Bible, you will want at least one other version for comparison. One of these should be an actual translation, not a paraphrase. A Bible dictionary is the next best tool you can own. It will give you background information to help unravel many questions. I like *The New Bible Dictionary*, but there are many others. Then consider a single-volume commentary for a section-by-section interpretation of Scripture through the eyes of biblical scholars (who work from various philosophies and methods of interpretation; do choose these with caution). *The New Bible Commentary* or *The International Bible Commentary* is a sound choice.

Before my separation, I thought I was too busy for any kind of Bible study. I owned a Revised Standard Version, a

Bible dictionary, and a Bible commentary, but I didn't make time to use them. The Holy Spirit showed me my error, and a friend encouraged me by saying, "It's OK to start small." Set up a short, specific, regular time for prayer and Bible study. As you feel more comfortable and see changes in your life, it will be easier to keep the schedule.

Here are some other practical tips to get you started:

- Pick a time when you are alert.
- Find a quiet place; unplug the phone or lock a door if you need to.
- Begin your Bible-reading time with prayer. Be quiet for a few moments, and allow God to speak to you about any sin or fault. Be honest as you respond in prayer to Him.
- Read slowly through one chapter or maybe two or three. (If you still don't know where to start, try Mark or John.) Ask yourself what it was all about, and then reread it. Some helpful questions include, What is the main subject of this passage? Who is speaking? What does this passage teach me about the Lord Jesus Christ? Is there a sin for me to confess, a command for me to obey, or a promise for me to claim?[12]
- Keep a notebook of your devotional time. Take brief notes and record what you are learning through the Scriptures, your thoughts, feelings, questions, joys, doubts, struggles, and God's answers to prayer. Journal writing can be a great tool, but it is not a command. If you don't like it, try something else.
- End your time by thanking God for what you have learned.

In a devotional time you will learn to love God with all your heart (Matt. 22:37) as you relate personally with

Him. But that's not enough: "The disadvantage of confining Bible study to devotional study is that it offers an unbalanced diet—too much milk, too little meat. It needs to be supplemented by other forms."[13] An in-depth study lets you love God with all your mind. Find an in-depth Bible study method that feels comfortable to you and capitalizes on your abilities. Here are some that can be used in private or in a group.

Topical or Thematic Study

Choose a topic or theme such as prayer, love, or sin. With your concordance you can look up some verses containing the word. With your dictionary and commentary you can gather all sorts of other information. This research can increase your wisdom and add to your knowledge.

Systematic Study

The Bible can be studied in great depth by looking specifically at books, chapters, paragraphs, verses, or words. By taking one chapter a day, you can intensively study the whole Bible in three years. You could even do it one paragraph a day—given enough time!

Inductive Bible Study

Inductive or logical reasoning can help you discover the meaning and principles of a passage or of an entire book.[14] After reading the section, you ask, "Who, what, when, why, where, and how?" Then think about the function and reason for the passage. Finally, ask, How does it relate to me personally?[15]

You might find it easier to begin in-depth Bible study if you join a group. There is discipline in the deadline of a regular weekly meeting: You need to get your homework done, and you need to show up. There is also joy in sharing and learning together. You can choose a small or large group—anything from a mixed Sunday school class to a casual day or evening get-together to the more structured Bible Study Fellowship International program. When I was separated I met weekly in a home on a weekday morning with six to eight other women for Bible study. Every one of us was struggling with difficult issues, everything from separation to bankruptcy to a wayward child to an abusive spouse. It was a constant joy to pray with one another, study God's Word, and learn together how we were to act as Christians.

WHY IS IT SO HARD TO GO TO CHURCH?

It had been easy for me to find excuses for not going to church regularly: The baby was sick, my toddler would cry if I left her in the nursery, I had to work, or I was too tired from working and Sunday was my day to rest. I asked a coworker who was separated if she went to church. She said, "I don't go very often. Sunday is the only day I have to be with my kids. Besides, it's always so boring." Many of us use excuses because we aren't motivated or inspired. You can, however, find time for public worship and fellowship if you choose to make church a priority in your life. If Sunday mornings are difficult, explore some of the other meeting times that are available. Once I decided to go back to church, a wonderful neighbor and I helped each other overcome our excuses. We shared a baby-sitter so we could leave our babies at home. We could take our toddlers because when they went to the toddler room together, they were no longer frightened.

Another neighbor said, "All they ever do in church is beg for money. I'm sick of hearing about why I should tithe. I'm not going to go anymore." The church has financial obligations, and God expects us to support His work (Mal. 3:8–10). Money is not the main topic of discussion in most churches, but sometimes that's all we hear because we aren't comfortable or well informed about how to give our money: We feel guilty. During my separation, even though my income was cut in half, I decided, for the first time in my life, to be obedient to God in this area. The first check I wrote each month was to my church. I could sit guilt-free through any sermon on tithing or any mention of the poor finances of the church. Because I knew I was being obedient and doing all that God required of me, I was no longer overly sensitive or offended.

I've also heard the excuse, "I don't go to church because I'm embarrassed. I don't have a husband to sit with anymore. What if I start to cry?" When I felt like that, I tried to keep in mind that though my painful circumstance of separation was visible, other people in the church hurt, too—their pains were just more hidden. Betty had another sad, but not uncommon reason for not going to church. One day she told me, "I never knew how people were going to react when they heard I was separated, so I just stopped going. Someone told me, 'You're a sinner and you'll never go to heaven unless you're reconciled with your husband.' Another woman said, 'You'd better take a look at yourself, honey, because your husband must have had a good reason to leave.'" The church should be a part of our healing process. Nevertheless, sometimes you might feel that people are too judgmental. Don't let the sins of others and their insensitivity stop you from worshiping God or from functioning as a member of His family. After all, it's a family in which *every* member needs help, in one form or another, to become more like Jesus.

WHY SHOULD I GO TO CHURCH?

When you became a Christian, you were born into God's family and automatically became a member of the body of Christ (1 Cor. 12:13). The Bible also pictures this fellowship as the bride of Christ (Eph. 5:22–29). You *can* succeed in this marriage! Your relationship is guaranteed and maintained by the Holy Spirit (1 Cor. 12:3). When you accepted Christ, God became your Father, and every other Christian believer in the world became your brother or sister in Christ. As a part of a spiritual family, you have privileges and responsibilities to your relatives.

In English, the word *church* can mean a Christian place of worship. However, in the New Testament, it never refers to a building. Usually, it means a local congregation of people.[16] Through time, we have come to refer to the local church as a visible, functioning portion of the one church that spans all time and places. Even though the members may sometimes fail, the church itself continues through the blood of Christ and power of the Holy Spirit. The first-century churches "were all *imperfect* churches made up of *imperfect* people who regularly came together because of their need for one another and their perfect Lord."[17] Despite the imperfections, it was, and still is, a privilege to meet together. In his book *Life Together*, Dietrich Bonhoeffer wrote, "Christians are privileged to live in visible fellowship with other Christians. It is by the grace of God that a congregation is permitted to gather visibly in this world to share God's Word and sacrament."[18]

Since the first century, the church has been a place to receive instruction and assistance through fellowship and prayer (including miracles), and a place to give God praise, worship, and service (Acts 2:42–47). It is where we receive spiritual supervision (1 Pet. 5:1–3), correction and discipline (Matt. 18:15–17), instruction and preparation for ministry (Eph. 4:12), and freedom to develop our spiritual gifts (1 Cor. 12). The gifts (jobs, talents, and desires) that the Holy Spirit gives us may bring us personal honor and achievement, but they are intended to be used cooperatively to benefit the whole church (Rom. 12:4–5).

After New Testament times, church life was formalized around certain rituals or sacraments. The Roman Catholic church today recognizes seven sacraments: confirmation, orders, matrimony, penance, extreme unction, baptism, and holy Communion. Protestant churches generally recognize only the last two as sacraments, though there are often forms and traditions associated with the others. The accepted "definition of a sacrament . . . is that of an outward and visible sign, ordained by Christ, setting forth and pledging an inward and spiritual blessing."[19] Baptism is a physical representation of the death and resurrection of Christ. It is linked with circumcision as an outward sign of separation from sin and membership in God's family (Col. 2:11–13). If you haven't been baptized, talk with your minister about it. It is also important for us as we share in fellowship with other believers to regularly remember our Savior's death in the sacrament of holy Communion (1 Cor. 11:24–26). It is a physical representation of the death of Christ and reminder of His return. It is linked with the Passover observance as an outward sign of inward obedience and recognition of God's historical act of salvation.[20] Now that's a blessing!

Perhaps you don't have a church and wonder how to go about finding one. First, pray about the matter. Don't be in any hurry. Ask friends and family members for their suggestions. Have a biblical understanding of the nature of the church. Discover some of the distinctive doctrines of denominations you are considering. If your first impression is good, attend for several weeks and try to get to know some people. If you are not satisfied, try elsewhere. Eventually, you will want to find a small group with which to pray and study the Scriptures. Also begin to look for ways in which you can help others in the church. Keep your expectations in perspective; realize that every church is imperfect because it is made up not of already perfected people but of believers on their way to becoming more like Christ.

We are meant to grow as we live in fellowship with other believers: "Try to look on the weekly experience not as *an activity you have joined* but as *a body of people to whom you belong.*"[21] Participation in a local church is not optional if you want to stay in touch with God—it is essential.

Your pain identifies you—your choices will direct you. The pain of broken communication may identify you. The communication between you and God is even more important than the communication between you and your spouse. Choose to stay in touch with Him through prayer, Bible study, and the church. Together they provide a solid, balanced support for your life, like the legs of a three-legged stool. They ensure that you will hear God when He calls and that He will answer you. Choose to give these activities high priority in your schedule. The result will be change—from surviving to thriving.

Dear Lord, thank You for always being available to me. Help me pray more effectively that I might know You more completely. Help me study Your Word with diligence that I might understand You more clearly. Help me to participate with Your family in a local church that I might worship You and serve others. In Jesus' name, Amen.

WHILE YOU'RE STAYING IN TOUCH WITH GOD, TAKE TIME TO CONSIDER...

1. Do you always feel like you want to communicate with God? Is it hard for you to pray? To study the Bible? To go to church?

2. Have you ever tried to manipulate God? Do you find it hard to know what to pray for?

3. What kind of results have you had when God has answered your prayers?

4. When is your most effective prayer time? Do you have a consistent daily devotional time? How does it affect your relationship with God?

5. Do you have an understandable version of the Bible? What is it? Do you like reading it?

6. What Bible study method are you using? What arrangements have you made for group or personal in-depth Bible study?

7. What kind of connection do you see between God and the local church?

8. Do you attend church now? If you are looking for a church, how will you know when you've found the right one?

9. Is there any particular activity of the church you'd like to be involved in? Choir, office help, visiting, maintenance, teacher, child care, elder, deacon?

10. Do you feel comfortable when money is discussed at church?

11. Have you been baptized? Do you take holy Communion?

12. What would you like to see happen in your prayer life, Bible study life, or church life?

NOTES

1. J. D. Douglas, ed., *The New Bible Dictionary* (Grand Rapids, Mich.: Eerdmans, 1971), p. 1021.

2. Oswald Chambers, *My Utmost for His Highest* (New York: Dodd, Mead, 1935), p. 241.

3. Lloyd John Ogilvie, *Praying with Power* (Ventura, Calif.: Regal Books, 1983), p. 23.

4. Peter M. Lord, *The 2959 Plan* (Titusville, Fla.: Agape Ministries, 1976), p. 14.

5. Paul E. Billheimer, *Destined for the Throne* (Fort Washington, Penn.: Christian Literature Crusade, 1975), p. 18.

6. Ibid.

7. Ben Patterson, *Waiting: Finding Hope When God Seems Silent* (Downers Grove, Ill.: InterVarsity Press, 1989), p. 12.

8. Haddon Robinson, *Jesus' Blueprint for Prayer* (Grand Rapids, Mich.: Radio Bible Class, 1989), p. 30.

9. Ibid.

10. "How to Study the Bible," The New King James Version of the Holy Bible: The Open Bible Expanded Edition (Nashville: Thomas Nelson, 1983), p. 8.

11. David Egner, *How Can I Know God Through His Book?* (Grand Rapids, Mich.: Radio Bible Class, 1988), p. 3.

12. "How to Study the Bible," p. 17.

13. John White, *The Fight* (Downers Grove, Ill.: InterVarsity Press, 1976), p. 47.

14. Ibid.

15. Robert M. Kachur, *The Complete Campus Companion* (Downers Grove, Ill.: InterVarsity Press, 1988), p. 227.

16. Douglas, *The New Bible Dictionary*, p. 228.

17. Martin R. De Haan II, *Who Needs the Church?* (Grand Rapids, Mich.: Radio Bible Class, 1990), p. 3.

18. Dietrich Bonhoeffer, *Life Together* (New York: Harper & Row, 1954), p. 18.

19. Douglas, *The New Bible Dictionary*, p. 1112.

20. Ibid., p. 750.

21. White, *The Fight*, p. 134.

CHAPTER NINE

Choose to Thrive

"Come look, Mommy!" my five-year-old daughter cried. "Something terrible has happened in the front yard."

I went to the window to see our apple tree lying on its side. The entire root ball was exposed to the rising sun. The hole where the roots belonged was enlarged, apparently dug up by an animal in the night.

"We need to replant it quick!" she announced. "Mommy, if we don't, it will die."

As I replaced the roots in the hole and firmly tapped down the dirt, I was pleased to see the tree stand tall once again. I placed the hose gently at its base. "Can I turn the water on now?" she asked.

"Very slowly," I said.

"Can I say a prayer for the tree, Mommy?"

"Of course, I think it can use all the help it can get."

We bowed our heads as if at a graveside: "Dear Lord, this tree got hurt real bad. Help us to take good care of it.

Please help it grow strong so it will make fruit for us to eat. Amen."

As I drove off to work that morning, I thought about the tree we had just replanted and my daughter's prayer. I had been just like that tree. Things were going along fine in my life when I was suddenly uprooted—I "got hurt real bad." I lay exposed to the elements and was ready to die, were it not for the Lord's touch. He came along and replanted me. The Lord fed and watered me through the power of prayer and His Word, and He sustained me through the support of my church. Through the power of the Holy Spirit, He kept me alive and, as promised, helped me to grow. I had hope that someday I, too, would be strong and bear fruit for the One who loved me, the One who had given me another chance to live.

SURVIVING OR THRIVING?

God's purpose for us is not that we merely survive but that we live an abundant, fruitful life that brings Him honor and glory. My separation exaggerated some problems that had always been present in my life and created some other entirely new ones: questions, grief, self-esteem, separation from God, sin, doubt, worry, uncertainty of God's promises, disobedience, change and stress, personality, loneliness, and poor communication. In this book I've suggested several ways to handle these problems. Perhaps you're like I was, though, and sometimes you still feel defeated or discouraged.

Recently, I found an old journal entry that reminded me of how I looked to God for the strength I needed. My neighbor called with an invitation to pick cherries from her backyard tree. "It's loaded. The fruit is just dropping off," Alisa said. "It's the most fruit this tree has ever had. I think it was those unexpected heavy rains we had last March. Who would have guessed that rain would be responsible for the best cherries ever?" I remembered that those rains in March had been unwelcome and had posed a threat. I wrote in my journal that I hoped God would use my "unexpected heavy rain" of separation to produce some spectacular fruit in me.

The Bible tells us we will be known by the fruit we bear. Fruit indicates the type and condition of the tree (Luke 6:43–44). Good trees, whether they are apple or fig trees, bear good fruit. But a weak or damaged tree cannot bear sweet fruit. I have learned that to be strong and to bear abundant good fruit as Christians, we must allow the Holy Spirit to fill us, and we must *abide* in Christ (John 15:5). I think of myself as a branch grafted into the tree or vine that is Christ and the Holy Spirit as the life-sustaining sap that keeps me growing there, enabling me to produce fruit.

To abide means "to reside with or to submit to." Because I continue to have my free will, spiritual growth is possible only as I cooperate with the Holy Spirit. The Holy Spirit prompts, I choose to respond to Him, and after my decision, He provides His power. Growth and fruit come because I know who God is, am intimately connected to Him (grafted in), and am controlled by His power. I am constantly choosing to abide (obey), and He is constantly filling (empowering).

I wanted to be like the prosperous tree described in Psalm 1 that was planted by the rivers of water, bringing forth its fruit in its season (v. 3). However, my roots were still shallow, like those of the young apple tree that we replanted. Only through the power of the Holy Spirit would I grow, sending roots down deep so that I couldn't be dug up easily.

WHO IS THE HOLY SPIRIT, AND
WHAT DOES HE DO?

In the King James Version of the Bible, the Holy Spirit is called the Holy Ghost. Modern translations prefer the word Spirit. No matter what He's called, this Person of the Trinity is often misunderstood. The Bible gives us information about who the Holy Spirit is, and when we get to know Him, we will love Him. He has a mind and a will of His own (Rom. 8:27; 1 Cor. 12:11); as God, He has always existed (Heb. 9:14); He is everywhere (Ps. 139:7); He has the very qualities of God the Father and God the Son: He is supreme (Gen. 1:2), powerful (Acts 1:8), holy and just (John 15:26; 16:8–9), loving (Rom. 5:5), and wise (Isa. 11:2).

Although God is one and cannot be divided, the mystery of God is that He is also three. Each person of the Trinity (Tri-Unity) has a specific function to play in our lives. Though we usually think of God the Father as the Creator, all of God was involved in creation (Father: Gen. 1:1; Son: Col. 1:15–16; Holy Spirit: Gen. 1:2; all: Gen. 1:26). Likewise, all of God was and is involved in the plan of salvation. The Bible leads us to see God the Father as the One who made the plan, God the Son as the One who obeyed the plan by dying for our sins, and God the Holy Spirit as the One who completes the plan by working in the lives of believers.

So where exactly is the Holy Spirit, and what is He doing? Jesus told His disciples when the Holy Spirit came upon them, they would have power to become His witnesses (Acts 1:8). The Spirit's authority and power were at work in the world before Pentecost, but He did not indwell believers until then (Acts 2:1–4). Though He is everywhere because He is God, we know Him best as

Christ's representative in our very lives. The Bible teaches that people become Christians through the work of the Holy Spirit (John 3:1–8). First, He prepares them by convicting them of sin (John 16:8). When they accept Christ, He gives them a new nature (2 Cor. 5:17). He dwells in Christians' hearts and minds, helping the newly created nature to mature and remain faithful.

The Holy Spirit *resides* in all Christians: "Your body is the temple of the Holy Spirit who is in you, whom you have from God" (1 Cor. 6:19). However, not all Christians are *filled* by the Holy Spirit. He fills believers as they praise and thank God and live in obedience to Christ (Eph. 5:18–21). It's so easy to say and so hard for us to do sometimes. The filling of the Holy Spirit is directly related to the lordship of Christ: "The filling does not mean that the Christian gets more of the Holy Spirit, but rather, He gets more of us!"[1] Filling is a result of a daily decision to allow Jesus to guide and direct us. It is placing Him at the hub of our lives, allowing Him full access to *every* aspect of our lives.

How will we know when we are filled by the Holy Spirit? One way is to see the "fruit of the Spirit" displayed in our lives—love, joy, peace, longsuffering, kindness, goodness, faithfulness, gentleness, and self-control (Gal. 5:22–23). These fruits are a result of what we have become through our relationship with God. We cannot produce a fruit simply by focusing on the fruit itself; we must focus on Christ. As the Holy Spirit helps us to obey and yield ourselves to Jesus as Lord of our lives (1 Cor. 12:3), we become more like Christ—more loving, joyful, peaceful, and so on. By these fruits, the world will see not only what you have or what you can do but who you are.

I wanted these fruits in my life, and I wanted freedom from the problems in my life: questions, doubts and worries, anger and bitterness. They were stunting my growth. As I remembered that Jesus promised that obedience to His words would reveal the truth and set me free, I began to rejoice in the wonder of God's plan: The Holy Spirit would make Jesus' promise a reality in my life. I looked forward to the filling of the Spirit who would be with me forever (John 14:16) and whose power would bring me peace (and all the other fruits) and freedom (Gal. 5:23).

HOW CAN I BEGIN TO LOVE?

The Holy Spirit began to change me in ways I never had thought possible. The Bible describes the victorious Christian life as one in which the believer continually walks in the Spirit (Gal. 5:16–18). Walking represents a moment-by-moment (step-by-step) submission to the Spirit's will and control, and yet freedom is the end result. I was free when I knew I was loved by God unconditionally, and when in turn I finally could love others, even those who had hurt me deeply.

The Bible has a lot to say about love. Jesus Himself agrees that love is the essence of obedience to God. Love God and love your neighbor. John writes, "God is love" (1 John 4:8). In 1 Corinthians 13, Paul describes fifteen concrete actions that demonstrate love. He finishes the passage by writing, "And now abide faith, hope, love, these three; but the greatest of these is love" (v. 13). Why is love so significant? The *faith* of Abraham and Moses is astonishing (Heb. 11:8–12, 17–19, 24–29). The *hope* of one day being known by God and seeing Him face-to-face is astonishing. Yet Paul says *love* is greater than either faith or hope. It is greater than any other talent or ability. Love is powerful and gives value and meaning to our actions.

Love can hurt us and heal us; it can change us and those around us; it can change the direction of our lives.

When we are filled with the Holy Spirit and become more like Christ, we can love as He loves—with the agape love of God (John 13:34–35). *Agape* is a Greek word for a special type of love, not having to do with affection or passion. As it expresses God's love for people, it shows God's nature, choice, and action.[2] It is an activity, not just a feeling or an attitude: "For God so loved the world that He *gave* His only begotten Son" (John 3:16, emphasis added). Ed Wheat says that agape love is "directed and fueled, not by the emotions, but by the will. Out of His own mighty nature, God supplies the resources for this love, and they are available to any life connected with His by faith in Jesus Christ."[3] "The love of God has been poured out in our hearts by the Holy Spirit," we learn in Romans 5:5.

During my separation, I realized for the first time in my life how much God loved and valued me, regardless of my sin and failure. When I was going the wrong way, He was patient with me when I least deserved it. Because I had experienced that undeserved love and acceptance from God, I was motivated to obey Him. He says, "Love one another as I have loved you" (John 15:12), not, "Wait until you feel like loving." I began to want to offer to my husband the same gift of unconditional love that God had offered me. Previously, all I had felt was anger, hate, and bitterness. You might wonder how I could even think about loving him. I assure you I had no intention of loving him as a lover or even as a friend, but I had read that as agape expresses Christian love for others, it "is not an impulse from feelings, it does not always run with the natural inclinations, nor does it spend itself only upon those for whom some affinity is discovered."[4] Despite my feelings, I could choose to obey God's command to love through action because "feelings are determined by actions—not the other way around."[5]

I knew exactly how God wanted me to act out my love. First, I needed to forgive my husband, and then, I needed to welcome his relationship with our children. Those were tough assignments. Forgiveness did not come quickly or easily for me. I was not instantly healed by Jesus like the man with the disabled hand, but I, too, believed God could do the impossible for me through the power of the Holy Spirit. God promised that if I obeyed Him, He would perfect His love in me (1 John 2:5). I did not despair or stop choosing to obey. The counselor I was seeing told me it usually takes years for separated people to forgive each other. As it turned out, it wasn't until I entered that last stage of grieving, acceptance, that I wholeheartedly forgave my husband. Your ability to forgive will depend on the depth of your pain and your spiritual development. Let the Holy Spirit, the Counselor Jesus promised, guide you (John 14:16).

HOW DO I FIND FREEDOM?

At first I wanted to forgive my husband on my terms, not on God's. I could not resolve my anger. I continued to express it through rage, repression, and redirection. How could God expect me to forgive my husband since he had not even said he was sorry? On the other hand, should I forgive him for my own sake, so I wouldn't be a slave to my deep anger and bitterness? I knew love and forgiveness would promote healing. Resentment and anger would take their toll on my physical and emotional well-being if I chose to hang on to them. But I just could not let go. Then the Holy Spirit began to lead me to the truth—that my bitterness, as a sin against God, was actually more serious than my husband's sin against me. I was ignoring how much God had forgiven me. Once again, God was calling me to do what was physically healthy and morally right. True forgiveness is an act of personally satisfying love because it frees us from bitterness, but it is also an act of agape love because it "releases another person from what he has done against us."⁶ When we release the wrong done to us and stop seeking revenge, we truly have forgiven.

Forgiveness comes when you *know* the facts and you are willing to let them go. When I accepted that it was no longer my responsibility to punish my husband for his sin, I could forgive. I knew that he would face God Himself, just as I had done. God is the ultimate Judge, and He will pay any vengeance due. Vengeance is Mine, says the Lord. I was not to repay anyone evil; I was to overcome evil with good (Rom. 12:17–21).

Despite our natural tendency to seek revenge, we can choose to love through the act of forgiveness. Then the Holy Spirit begins to work in our lives, providing the power we need. When we genuinely forgive, our lives will be free from hatred, blame, bitterness, anger, and revenge.

You may be saying, "I want to forgive my spouse, but I can't change the way I feel. I can't change the past." Don't be a slave to the past. Indeed, I found that nothing could change the past, but forgiveness allowed me to heal, complete the grieving process, and move on with my life. Ed Wheat says, "To forgive is to say good-by forever to the pain of the past and to be rid of its effects in the present."⁷ Accept the power the Holy Spirit offers. When He fills you, He will provide the strength you need to forgive—or to wait to forgive. You will be free as you choose to obey.

You may be saying, "I'd like to forgive my spouse, but I don't think I can ever feel any forgiveness after what happened." Don't be a slave to your feelings. Forgiveness, like love, is an action, not a feeling. When we are filled with the Holy Spirit and become more like Christ, we can forgive as Christ forgave. If anyone had the right to *feel* bitter, it was Jesus: He was rejected, falsely accused, and nailed to a cross. Yet He *said*, "Father, forgive them" (Luke 23:34). We are commanded to forgive as He forgave (Col. 3:13). When we choose to accept another person with forgiveness and mercy, we are following His example.

HOW DO I PURSUE PEACE?

Jesus said He came to give peace that is different from the world's (John 14:27). Oswald Chambers observed, "There are times when our peace is based upon ignorance, but when we awaken to the facts of life, inner peace is impossible unless it is received from Jesus—it is a peace which comes from looking into His face."[8] The Old Testament Hebrew word for peace means "completeness, soundness, well-being." It relates to physical and spiritual situations and relationships, and it is associated with righteousness and truth, never wickedness.[9] The Greek word used in the New Testament depends on this breadth of meaning. Christ came as the Prince of Peace (Isa. 9:6) to make peace between God and you in the present and to bring order to the world in the future. Peace is God's gift and work, but each believer is urged to pursue this peace (1 Pet. 3:11). How could I be an example or a messenger of this peace when I was not at peace with myself or with my husband? As I continued to follow the Holy Spirit's leading regarding my need to

make peace with my husband and welcome his relationship with our children, I discovered that love through
forgiveness was the way to peace, just as it was the way
to freedom.

You will remember earlier that I said Crystal was going
to stay at my house for two weeks while she looked for a
new place to live. We had many heart-to-heart talks during that time. I'll never forget one of those conversations.

My husband had just driven off with the children for
the weekend. "It's so nice to see your husband coming to
pick them up," said Crystal. "It must make you feel good,
knowing he makes time to be with them."

"To be real honest," I replied, "I'm not sure what they
need him for. I do everything for them now. I've thought
of moving away so I wouldn't have to involve him in our
lives. Whenever he comes around, I feel like I'm on an
emotional roller coaster—and I want to get off!"

"But they're so lucky to have a dad who cares. Don't
ruin it for them. My dad left when I was three—the same
age as your daughter. I don't remember anything about his
living with me and my mom. I've seen him only a couple
of times in my life, though I do talk to him on the phone
every now and then. I've never had any time with
him . . . time to get to know what kind of a person he really is."

"Do you feel your mom and dad love you?"

"Well . . . maybe," she whispered. Her sad eyes filled
with tears. "I've never heard my mom say one nice thing
about him. She's tried to make me hate the man that I
most want to love—he's my father, after all. I think I've
really missed something. You've tried to talk to me about
God's love, but it's hard for me to understand. The only
love I've ever known is critical and demeaning. What kind
of love is that?"

As she sobbed, I held her tightly. *No wonder she left home at sixteen and began to look for relationships with older men. If I continue to live my life filled with anger and bitterness, will my children end up lost and confused like Crystal?*

When she left me, I prayed, "God, I don't want my children to suffer. I don't want to hate anymore, but I don't know how to stop. You know I can't do it myself. I need Your help to replace my selfish feelings with Your unselfish love and forgiveness."

It was easy for me to believe in a God who loved me like a father because I had never doubted my father's love for me. How could I want to take away from my children the chance to get to know their father? Safety was not the issue; I knew my husband was responsible and would not deliberately harm them. Yet I knew if I chose to involve him in our lives, it would mean I would have to share the children even when I didn't want to on holidays and vacations.

The issues you are facing may be different, but you must respond to what God is asking you to do. You will begin to grow and produce the fruit of peace in your life when you express the agape love of God through obedient actions and forgiveness. Peace is the proof that you are right with God because you are at liberty to turn your mind to Him instead of yourself or your problems.

I remember the day God finally freed me. The last thing on my mind was having a heavy-duty conversation with the Lord. Yet, all alone in a spa Jacuzzi, the Holy Spirit chose to fill me with the strength I needed to wholeheartedly forgive my husband. I remember opening my time of prayer by thanking God for being so patient with me and for helping me grow over the past two years. There was no audible voice through the sound of the bubbles, but I was aware of the Holy Spirit speaking to me, "Since God's been loving, forgiving, and patient with you, Jan, are you ready to offer the same to your husband?" At that moment I had strength I'd never had before. I listed every wrong I felt my husband had done to me, and I chose to forgive them one by one. I left that spa room warm and glowing on both the inside and the outside. I had an inner peace I'd never experienced before.

The minute I forgave my husband, I experienced peace, but I found that if I wanted to continue experiencing that peace, I needed to learn how to forgive repeatedly. Not surprisingly, conflict still arose as I continued to interact with my husband. I could choose to enter once again into the cycle of revenge, or I could choose to forgive. I can honestly say, since that day in the Jacuzzi, I have never again had the desire to seek revenge. When I keep the slate clean and choose to forgive, I am free to produce the fruit of peace. So can you!

I discovered that I could act differently. When the children came back from visiting their dad, I didn't pry for information. I no longer was jealous of the things they did together, nor did I feel the need to compete. I knew they needed to feel his love and develop their relationship with him. I could allow that freely at last.

I had known a new friend for only two weeks when she said, "You are different from most separated women I know. You don't berate your husband. You aren't pleased about what he's done, but you actually have some kind things to say about him." Someone else could actually see the fruit of kindness in my words. Not a patient person by nature, I was amazed to see my attitude change as well as my words.

I became excited to see what fruit God would produce next. I was overjoyed when joy appeared! For over a year I had struggled with the memories of my marriage. Then I realized I could relinquish even my memories to the Lord. He began to reassure me and validate my memories of past joys. In the midst of my sorrow, I began to experience joy in unexpected places: going to work, looking at old pictures, doing yard work, and going to church. The fruit of joy was definitely God's work, not mine!

WHAT CAN I DO NOW?

A child can be a great teacher.

"Mommy, did you know that a seed needs four things to grow? Soil, water, sunshine, and oxygen."

"Is that right?" I responded.

"Mommy, I'm growing a seed in a cup at school, and when I bring it home, I'll make you a deal, OK?"

"What's that?"

"I'll do the soil and water . . . and you do the sunshine and oxygen."

"Honey, there are certain things that I can do, but sunshine and oxygen aren't on the list. God is the only One who can do that part."

"Well, I guess I better let Him do it then."

I've spent a lot of time discussing what you can do in the midst of your separation—the choices you can make. I've also talked about what God can do in the midst of your separation—change you. You have a part to play, and so does He. As you begin to cooperate with Him, you will see that waiting while separated can be a rich time that produces sweet, abundant fruit in your life.

I had even more than fruit in my life, though. An old friend of our family came to me after church one Sunday and said, "Jan, I see a renewed faith in you. It probably was there all the time . . . just not attended to." It was true. I did have a faith to call my own. I knew who God was, and I chose to put my trust in Him. I had hope, too. I realized that being married wouldn't make me a whole person; Jesus would. My hope was no longer in the restoration of my marriage but in Jesus and His power to change me. I also had "the greatest of these," God's love to share with the world.

Waiting on the Lord doesn't mean sitting back and waiting on everything and anything until your circumstances change, your separation is over, or your prayer finally is answered. It means taking action based on what you know about who God is. When you come to know God not only for what He can do for you but for who He wants to be for you and your spouse, you can take action. When you come to know God not only for what He can do for you but for what He can make of you and your spouse, you can take action. And the loving actions will lead to peace and freedom. Oswald Chambers wrote, "God will never reveal more truth about Himself until you have obeyed what you know already."[10] When you take obedient actions based on what you know about who God is, you can know the truth, and the truth will make you free (John 8:32). That's God's promise!

My good friend Norma, after three years of separation, said, "All the pain and suffering I've been through has been worth it because now I know who God is. I don't know if I would have discovered Him any other way. One thing I've learned is how precious each day is. God has proved Himself faithful to help me get through my days one at a time. Since I can't live more than one at a time, what more could I ever need?"

Your pain identifies you—your choices will direct you. There is pain in growing. You will feel growing pains when you choose to obey, especially when you don't feel like it. But when you take action based on what you know about who God is, you will be free—free from sin and free to depend on God completely. His power will keep you alive and growing.

You will thrive when you choose to allow the Holy Spirit to empower you. You cannot live the Christian life in your own strength (John 15:5). It takes the power of God to change your attitudes, your outlook on your circumstances, and the direction of your life. Stop struggling to survive. The Holy Spirit will fill you with the strength and power you need to thrive. The greatest evidence of His power is seen in the change He brings about in lives. Take Him at His word (Rom. 8:6), and you will be free and have peace as you wait through the uncertainty of your separation.

> *Dear Lord, only now can I thank You for the heavy rain of my separation because I see a purpose in it. Help me to make the choices that allow You to fill me so I may love with Your agape love and forgive as You do. I have faith in You, hope that You will give me Your peace, and confidence that I am free—all because of Your great love for me. Help me to continue to wait with that assurance. In Jesus' name, Amen.*

WHILE YOU'RE THRIVING, TAKE TIME TO CONSIDER . . .

1. What problems in your life have been exaggerated by your separation? What new ones have been created?

2. Do you ever feel defeated in trying to live out your Christian life? Why?

3. What do you need to be freed from?

4. Do you need to forgive someone? What's stopping you?

5. What do you understand the function and activity of the Holy Spirit to be?

6. Have you been indwelt by the Holy Spirit? Filled by the Holy Spirit? How will you know?

7. Do you have spiritual fruits in your life? Which ones? Can other people see them?

8. Have you had growing pains? How long did they last?

9. Based on what you know about who God is, what loving actions can you take right now while you are waiting?

10. Are you willing to take loving actions, even though you don't feel like it? Even if your spouse continues to seek revenge?

11. Do you believe you are free in Christ? How have you experienced that freedom?

12. Do you believe you can have inner peace? Do you need to wait, or is God calling you to act now?

NOTES

1. The New King James Version of the Holy Bible: The Open Bible Expanded Edition (Nashville: Thomas Nelson, 1983), p. 1163.

2. W. E. Vine, *An Expository Dictionary of New Testament Words* (London: Oliphants, 1965), p. LOV-21.

3. Ed Wheat, M.D., and Gloria Okes Perkins, *Love Life for Every Married Couple* (Grand Rapids, Mich.: Zondervan, 1980), p. 119.

4. Vine, *An Expository Dictionary of New Testament Words*, p. LOV-21.

5. Wheat and Perkins, *Love Life for Every Married Couple*, p. 214.

6. Martin De Haan, "Forgiveness," *Times of Discovery* (Grand Rapids, Mich.: Radio Bible Class), July 1992, p. 1.

7. Wheat and Perkins, *Love Life for Every Married Couple*, p. 200.

8. Oswald Chambers, *My Utmost for His Highest* (New York: Dodd, Mead, 1935), p. 239.

9. J. D. Douglas, ed., *The New Bible Dictionary* (Grand Rapids, Mich.: Eerdmans, 1971), p. 956.

10. Chambers, *My Utmost for His Highest*, p. 284.

Bibliography

Billheimer, Paul E. *Destined for the Throne*. Fort Washington, Penn.: Christian Literature Crusade, 1975. Reprint. Minneapolis, Minn.: Bethany House, 1983.

Bonhoeffer, Dietrich. *Life Together*. New York: Harper & Row, 1954.

Bruce, F. F., general ed. *The International Bible Commentary*, rev. ed. Grand Rapids, Mich.: Zondervan, 1986.

Burns, Bob. *Recovery from Divorce*. Nashville: Thomas Nelson, 1992.

Burns, Bob, and Tom Whiteman. *The Fresh Start Divorce Recovery Workbook*. Nashville: Oliver-Nelson, 1992.

Carter, Dr. Les. *The Prodigal Spouse*. Nashville: Thomas Nelson, 1990.

Carter, Dr. Les, and Dr. Frank Minirth. *The Anger Workbook*. Nashville: Thomas Nelson, 1993.

Chambers, Oswald. *My Utmost for His Highest*. New York: Dodd, Mead, 1935.

Chapman, Gary. *Hope for the Separated*. Chicago: Moody Press, 1982.

Conway, Jim. *Men in Mid-Life Crisis*. Elgin, Ill.: David C. Cook, 1978.

Conway, Jim and Sally. *When One Mate Wants Out*. Grand Rapids, Mich.: Zondervan, 1992.

Conway, Sally. *You and Your Husband's Mid-Life Crisis*. Elgin, Ill.: David C. Cook, 1980.

De Haan, Kurt. *Can Anyone Really Know for Sure?* Grand Rapids, Mich.: Radio Bible Class, 1987.

———. *How Does God Keep His Promises?* Grand Rapids, Mich.: Radio Bible Class, 1989.

De Haan, Kurt, ed. *Our Daily Bread*. Grand Rapids, Mich.: Radio Bible Class.

De Haan, Martin. "Forgiveness." *Times of Discovery*, July 1992. Grand Rapids, Mich.: Radio Bible Class.

————. "Waiting in Line." *Times of Discovery*, December 1992. Grand Rapids, Mich.: Radio Bible Class.

De Haan, Martin R., II. *How Can I Feel Good About Myself?* Grand Rapids, Mich.: Radio Bible Class, 1988.

————. *Who Needs the Church?* Grand Rapids, Mich.: Radio Bible Class, 1990.

Dobson, James. *Love Must Be Tough*. Dallas: Word, 1983.

Doheny, Kathleen. "Fear of Flying: 1 in 6 Are in White-Knuckle Club." *Los Angeles Times*, October 25, 1992.

Douglas, J. D., ed. *The New Bible Dictionary*. Grand Rapids, Mich.: Eerdmans, 1971.

Egner, Dave. *What Can I Do with My Worry?* Grand Rapids, Mich.: Radio Bible Class, 1992.

Egner, David. *How Can I Know God Through His Book?* Grand Rapids, Mich.: Radio Bible Class, 1988.

Guthrie, Donald, and J. A. Motyer, eds. *The New Bible Commentary*, rev. ed. Grand Rapids, Mich.: Eerdmans, 1970.

Hemfelt, Robert, Frank Minirth, and Paul D. Meier. *Love Is a Choice*. Nashville: Thomas Nelson, 1989.

Henry, Matthew. *Commentary on the Whole Bible*. Grand Rapids, Mich.: Zondervan, 1961.

Hoffman, Mark S., ed. *The World Almanac and Book of Facts 1992*. New York: St. Martin's Press, 1991.

Jackson, Tim. *How Can I Live with My Loss?* Grand Rapids, Mich.: Radio Bible Class, 1992.

————. *When Help Is Needed*. Grand Rapids, Mich.: Radio Bible Class, 1993.

Jones, Thomas. *Sex & Love When You're Single Again*. Nashville: Oliver-Nelson, 1990.

Kachur, Robert M. *The Complete Campus Companion*. Downers Grove, Ill.: InterVarsity Press, 1988.

Keirsey, David, and Marilyn Bates. *Please Understand Me*. Del Mar, Calif.: Prometheus Nemesis Books, 1978.

Kübler-Ross, Elisabeth. *On Death and Dying*. New York: Macmillan, 1969.

Lord, Peter M. *The 2959 Plan*. Titusville, Fla.: Agape Ministries, 1976.

Lush, Jean. *Emotional Phases of a Woman's Life*. Old Tappan, N.J.: Fleming H. Revell, 1990.

McDowell, Josh. *A Ready Defense*. San Bernardino, Calif.: Here's Life Publishers, 1990.

McLuhan, M. G. *Marriage and Divorce: God's Call, God's Compassion*. Wheaton, Ill.: Tyndale, 1991.

Mehren, Elizabeth. "Family Feuds." *Los Angeles Times*, September 16, 1992.

Munger, Robert Boyd. *My Heart Christ's Home*. Downers Grove, Ill.: InterVarsity Press, 1986.

The New King James Version of the Holy Bible: The Open Bible Expanded Edition. Nashville: Thomas Nelson, 1983.

Noll, Mark A. "The Agony and Ecstasy of Waiting." *Christianity Today*, November 23, 1992.

Ogilvie, Lloyd John. *Praying with Power*. Ventura, Calif.: Regal Books, 1983.

The One Year Bible. Wheaton, Ill.: Tyndale, 1985.

Patterson, Ben. *Waiting: Finding Hope When God Seems Silent*. Downers Grove, Ill.: InterVarsity Press, 1989.

Petersen, J. Allan. *The Myth of the Greener Grass*. Wheaton, Ill.: Tyndale, 1983.

Powell, John. *Why Am I Afraid to Tell You Who I Am?* Niles, Ill.: Argus Communications, 1969.

Richmond, Gary. *The Divorce Decision*. Dallas: Word, 1988.

Robinson, Haddon. *Jesus' Blueprint for Prayer*. Grand Rapids, Mich.: Radio Bible Class, 1989.

Sanders, J. Oswald. *Lonely But Never Alone*. Grand Rapids, Mich.: Radio Bible Class, 1991.

Sarnoff, Irving and Suzanne. *Love-Centered Marriage in a Self-Centered World*. New York: Hemisphere Publishing, 1989.

Smoke, Jim. *Growing Through Divorce*. Eugene, Oreg.: Harvest House, 1976.

Swindoll, Charles. *Three Steps Forward, Two Steps Back*. Nashville: Thomas Nelson, 1980.

"Taking Charge of Life's Changes." *Adapting to Stress: Healthtrac—Start Taking Charge*. Seattle: The Hope Heart Institute, 1989.

Talley, Jim. *Reconcilable Differences: Mending Broken Relationships*. Nashville: Thomas Nelson, 1985.

Vanauken, Sheldon. *A Severe Mercy: Davy's Edition*. New York: Harper & Row, 1980.

Vine, W. E. *An Expository Dictionary of New Testament Words*. London: Oliphants, 1965.

Wheat, Ed. M.D., and Gloria Okes Perkins. *Love Life for Every Married Couple*. Grand Rapids, Mich.: Zondervan, 1980.

White, John. *The Fight*. Downers Grove, Ill.: InterVarsity Press, 1976.

Whiteman, Thomas. *Innocent Victims*. Nashville: Thomas Nelson, 1992.

Whyte, Martin King. *Dating, Mating and Marriage*. New York: Aldine de Gruyter, 1990.

Worden, William J. *Grief Counseling and Grief Therapy*. New York: Springer, 1991.

Zodhiates, Spiros. *May I Divorce and Remarry?* Chattanooga, Tenn.: AMG Publishers, 1989.